JOKELOPEDiA

The Biggest, Best, Silliest, Dumbest Joke Book Ever

Compiled by

Ilana Weitzman, Eva Blank, Alison Benjamin,
Rosanne Green, and Lisa Sparks

Illustrations by
Mike Wright

WORKMAN PUBLISHING • NEW YORK

T0018835

Thank-Yous

☆ ☆ ☆

We wanted this collection of jokes to be the biggest, best, dopiest, silliest, dumbest one on the planet. But that wouldn't have been possible without a lot of help from our friends.

The first edition was collected by Ilana Weitzman, Eva Blank, and Rosanne Green, with help from Cy Strom, Michael Redhill, Greg Ioannou, Laura Siberry, Suzanne Brandreth, Vivien Leong, Jane Somerville, Jill Byrant, Sam McKay, Camilla Dietrich, and Jill Kopelman.

The second edition was prepared with help from Beth Doty and Megan Nicolay at Workman, and Andrea Battiston and Greg Ioannou at Colborne Communications. We'd like to particularly thank Barb Webb, who did a lot of the initial planning for how to make the book even funnier. Kids from all over North America sent in some of the coolest jokes in the book and we'd like to thank them. And extra-special thanks to all our joke guinea pigs who had to spend months listening to our worst groaners and stinkiest wisecracks.

This third edition would not have been successful if not for my coworkers at Colborne Communications and Iguana Books, who not only helped with jokes but also listened, laughed, and groaned (more often than not) at my attempts to be funny. And thanks to all my friends and family members for keeping me in stitches with their jokes in the hopes of being put in the book!

Lisa Sparks

Copyright © 2000 by Somerville House, 2006 by Key Porter and Workman Publishing, 2013, 2016 by Workman Publishing Co., Inc., a subsidiary of Hachette Book Group, Inc.

All rights reserved. No portion of this book may be reproduced—mechanically, electronically, or by any other means, including photocopying—without written permission of the publisher.

Library of Congress Cataloging-in-Publication Data is available.

ISBN 978-0-7611-8997-8

Cover Design by Paul Gamarello
Interior Design by Janet Vicario with Munira Al-Khalili

Workman books are available at special discounts when purchased in bulk for premiums and sales promotions as well as for fundraising or educational use. Special editions or book excerpts can also be created to specification. For details, please contact special.markets@hbgusa.com.

Workman Publishing Co., Inc., a subsidiary of Hachette Book Group, Inc.
1290 Avenue of the Americas
New York, NY 10104
workman.com

Distributed in Europe by Hachette Livre, 58 rue Jean Bleuzen, 92 178 Vanves Cedex, France.
Distributed in the United Kingdom by Hachette Book Group, UK,
Carmelite House, 50 Victoria Embankment, London EC4Y 0DZ.

WORKMAN is a registered trademark of Workman Publishing Co., Inc., a subsidiary of Hachette Book Group, Inc.

Printed in China on responsibly sourced paper.
First printing August 2016
15 14 13 12 11 10 9 8 7 6

So you want to be Funny?

Welcome to *Jokelopedia*. We see it as a big, thick reminder of the lighter side of life and hope you use it to make your friends and family groan and smile— although not necessarily in that order.

Do you know what a shaggy-dog joke is? Have you ever seen a chicken cross the road? Well, you will soon. Would you like to make your classmates laugh so hard at lunchtime that milk comes out of their noses? Do you feel like wowing them with humor history from the Three Stooges or *The Simpsons*? Do you want to tell the funniest jokes, learn how your favorite comedians made a living before comedy, how sitcoms came to be, and how to make people laugh, *your* way? If so, this is the book for you.

With contributions from kids, tricky tongue twisters, long long jokes, short short jokes, and general crazy ideas and tips, this just might be the funniest book ever.

No joke.

CONTENTS

TALL TAILS
Animals with Attitude

> Did you hear the one about the giraffe?

Did you hear the one about the lion who ate clowns?

You'll roar.

What do you call a cat who eats a lemon?

A sourpuss.

Why shouldn't you shortchange a skunk?

It's bound to make a stink.

What did the judge say when the skunk came in to testify?

"Odor in the court!"

> Oh, well, it's way over your head.

EAT

There were these two buddies out walking their dogs, one with a Doberman pinscher and the other with a Chihuahua, when they smelled something delicious coming from a nearby restaurant.

The guy with the Doberman says to his friend, "Let's go over to that restaurant and get something to eat." The guy with the Chihuahua says, "We can't go in there. We've got dogs with us."

The buddy with the Doberman says, "Just follow my lead." He puts on a pair of dark glasses and walks into the restaurant, when the restaurant owner comes up and says, "Sorry, pal, no pets allowed."

The man with the Doberman replies, "You don't understand. This is my Seeing Eye dog."

The owner, skeptical, says, "A Doberman pinscher?"

The Doberman's master says, "Yes, they're using them now—they're very good and they protect me from robbers, too." The owner says, "Come on in."

When the man with the Chihuahua sees this, he puts on a pair of dark glasses and starts to walk in. Once again the restaurant owner says, "Sorry, pal, no pets allowed."

The guy with the Chihuahua says, "You don't understand. This is my Seeing Eye dog."

"A Chihuahua?" says the owner.

The man with the dog replies, "A Chihuahua? They gave me a Chihuahua?!" ☆

2

ha-ha!

What do you call an overweight cat?

A flabby tabby.

Why was the rabbit so unhappy?

She was having a bad hare day.

How do you catch a squirrel?

Climb a tree and act like a nut.

3

THE MAKING OF A COMEDIAN

Step 1: What Is a Joke Made Of?

What makes a joke a joke? What is the difference between the biggest, best, silliest, dumbest, dopiest joke ever and one that falls totally flat?

First is the *setup*. Launch right into the joke. Make sure you know the whole thing backward and forward—there's nothing quite as embarrassing as realizing you forgot the funny part.

Next is *timing*. Comedic timing is a skill that takes lots and lots of practice to perfect. Don't rush through your joke. Give your audience time to figure it out. But don't wait too long or they'll lose interest.

Finally: the *punch line*. This is the last part of a joke—the part you've been building up to, whether you've been telling a long shaggy-dog joke (more on those later!) or a short-'n'-sweet riddle. It's the funny part. Tell it loudly and firmly. Don't laugh in the middle of it or you'll ruin the suspense. Leave that up to your audience. The punch line should have an effect like its name—a punch of silliness, right to the funny bone.

The Care and Feeding of King Cobras by I. Will Havastroke

BOOK TITLES We'd Love to See:

Are You a Liar? by I.M. Knott

World Travel by I.M. Tyred and Jett L'Agg

Fibbing Effectively by Liza Lott

101 Ways to Miss a Day of School by Ben Barphin

101 Hot 'n' Spicy Meals by Tung Payne

The Art of Flossing by Dr. D. Kay

Getting Dirty by Anita Bath

Junk Food by Chip Eaton

The Ways of Poker by Ahmal Inn

Counting by Juan Toothree

Outdoor Furniture by Pat T. O'Chairs

Clean Bathrooms by Ty D. Boal

4

A woman walks into a diner carrying a dog under her arm. She puts the dog on the counter and announces that the dog can talk. The woman says she has $100 she's willing to bet anyone who says he can't. The head cook quickly takes the bet, and the dog's owner looks at the dog and asks, "What's the thing on top of this building that keeps the rain out?"

The dog answers, *"Roof."* The cook says, "Who are you kidding? I'm not paying."

The dog's owner says, "Double or nothing, and I'll ask him something else." The cook agrees and the owner turns to her dog and asks, "Who was the greatest baseball player ever?"

The dog answers with a muffled *"Ruth."*

With that the cook picks them both up and tosses them out on the street. As they bounce on the sidewalk in front of the diner, the dog looks at his owner and says, *"DiMaggio?"* ☆

Funny Fact

Did you know it takes 17 muscles to smile and 43 to frown?

What kind of language do porcupines speak?

Spine language.

How did the tree feel after the beaver left?

Gnawed so good.

A man sitting in a movie theater notices that there is a bear sitting next to him. Finally he turns to the bear and says, "Aren't you a bear?" The bear nods, so the man says, "So what are you doing at the movies?" The bear says, "Well, I liked the book." ☆

What did the baby porcupine say to the cactus?

"Is that you, Mommy?"

One day, a cat died of natural causes and went to heaven. There he met Saint Peter at the Pearly Gates. Saint Peter said to the cat, "You have lived a good life, and if there is any way I can make your stay in heaven more comfortable, please let me know."

Knock, knock.
Who's there?
The interrupting cow.
The interrup—
MOOOOOOOOOOOOOOO!

The cat thought for a moment and said, "All my life I have lived with a poor family and have had to sleep on a hard wooden floor."

"Say no more," Saint Peter replied, and poof! A wonderful, fluffy pillow appeared.

A few days later, six mice were killed in a tragic farming accident and went to heaven. Again there was Saint Peter to greet them with the same offer. The mice answered, "All of our lives we have been chased. We have had to run from cats, dogs, and even women with brooms. We are tired of running. Do you think we could have roller skates so that we don't have to run anymore?" Instantly each mouse was fitted with a beautiful pair of roller skates.

About a week later, Saint Peter stopped by to see the cat and found him snoozing on the pillow. He gently woke the cat and asked, "How are things for you since coming to heaven?"

The cat stretched, yawned, and replied, "It's wonderful here—even better than I could have expected. Especially those meals-on-wheels you've been sending by—those are the best!" ✩

Jane asks Mark: "What do you call a deer with no eyes?"
Mark shrugs and says, "No-eye deer."

What type of shoes do bears wear?

None. They go bear foot.

What do you get from a pampered cow?

Spoiled milk.

What do you get when you cross a mountain lion with a parrot?

I don't know, but when it talks, you'd better listen!

Why was the cat so small?

Because it drank only condensed milk!

7

Two women are out hiking when a bear starts chasing them. They climb a tree, but the bear starts climbing up the tree after them. The first woman gets her sneakers out of her backpack and puts them on. The second woman says, "What are you doing?"

The first woman says, "I figure when the bear gets close to us, we'll jump down and make a run for it."

The second woman says, "Are you crazy? You can't outrun a bear."

The first woman says, "I don't have to outrun the bear. . . . I only have to outrun you!" ✫

Why do Cows have bells?

Their horns don't work.

Where do monkeys pick up wild rumors?

What did the 500-pound canary say as he walked down the street?

"Here, kitty, kitty, kitty."

Why aren't leopards any good at hide-and-seek?

Because they're always spotted.

Why do you have to be careful when it rains cats and dogs?

To make sure you don't step in a poodle.

Why should you be careful when playing against a team of big cats?

They might be cheetahs.

While walking along the street, a man saw a sign that said: TALKING DOG FOR SALE, $10. The man couldn't believe his ears when the dog said, "Please buy me. I'm a great dog. I played professional football. I was even nominated most valuable player."

"That dog really *does* talk!" the man gasped. "Why in the world do you want to sell him for only ten dollars?"

"He never played professional football," said the dog's owner, "and I can't stand liars." ☆

Through the apevine.

Saturday Night Live

Saturday Night Live began in 1975 as a showcase for talented young comedians. A television producer named Lorne Michaels created the show as a series of comedic skits, called sketches, that would air live. Although each show is loosely scripted and rehearsed, the live taping encourages improvisation and quick thinking among the cast.

A cast of comedians plays different characters in the sketches during the 90-minute show, which airs around 11:30 p.m. on Saturday nights in the Eastern time zone. Each week, a celebrity host—usually a movie or TV star—opens the show with a monologue and appears in a few skits, and a popular music group performs a few songs on the air as well.

SNL, as it is commonly known, has launched the careers of many comedians and comic actors, including several of those featured in this book. Adam Sandler, Tina Fey, and Will Ferrell all performed on SNL. Many comics who appear on the show create distinctive characters for their skits— Mike Myers's Wayne Campbell and "Wayne's World," for example. SNL writers and actors pay close attention to current events in order to shape the show. For more than 40 years, the show has been the place to be for up-and-coming comic talent and a witty look at what's happening in the world.

What do you call a cat who can bowl?

An alley cat.

BEHIND THE PUNCH LINE:

Sitcoms

A *situation comedy*, or sitcom for short, is a television show format that features a humorous conflict and resolution in each episode. We watch sitcoms because the characters get themselves tangled up in the most ridiculous situations! Often, it's extra funny because the audience knows exactly what's going on, while the characters involved are clueless.

TV producers who create sitcoms hire comedy writers to think up zany scenarios and write funny lines for the show's script. Since there are a variety of characters to work with, these writers have a flexibility that stand-up comedians don't have: They can make the characters trade lines back and forth, blurting out unexpected quips or funny comebacks with very funny results.

We showcase classic shows like *Seinfeld*, *I Love Lucy*, and *Full House* in *Jokelopedia*. Watch for them!

What do you call a cat who's been thrown in the dryer?
Fluffy.

What do you call a cat who gets thrown in the dryer and is never found again?
Socks.

What did the cat get on the test?
A purr-fect score.

What do you give to an injured pig?
Oinkment.

What animal has more lives than a cat?
A frog. It croaks every night.

What has six eyes but can't see?
Three blind mice.

What do you get when you cross Lassie with a rose?
A collie flower.

One day an out-of-work mime is visiting the zoo, and he figures he'll try to earn some money performing. Unfortunately, as soon as he starts to draw a crowd, a zookeeper grabs him and drags him into his office.

The zookeeper explains to the mime that the zoo's most popular attraction, a gorilla, has died suddenly and the keeper fears that attendance at the zoo will fall off. He offers the mime a job to dress up as the gorilla until they can get another one. The mime accepts.

The next morning the mime puts on a gorilla suit and enters the cage before the crowd arrives. He discovers that it's a great job. He can sleep all he wants, play, and make fun of people, and he draws bigger crowds than he ever did as a mime.

However, eventually the crowds tire of him and he gets bored with swinging on tires. He begins to notice that the people are paying more attention to the lion in the cage next to his. Not wanting to lose the attention of his audience, he climbs to the top of his cage, crawls across a divider, and dangles from the top of the lion's cage. Of course, this makes the lion furious, but the crowd loves it. At the end of the day the zookeeper comes and gives the mime a raise for being such a good attraction.

This goes on for some time. The mime keeps taunting the lion, the crowds grow larger, and the mime's salary keeps going up. Then one terrible day while he is dangling over the furious lion, he slips and falls. The mime is terrified. The lion

SHHH!

12

gathers himself and prepares to pounce. The mime is so scared that he begins to run round and round the cage with the lion close behind. Finally, the mime starts screaming and yelling "Help me! Help me!" but the lion is quick and pounces. The mime soon finds himself flat on his back, looking up at the angry lion, who growls, "Shut up, you idiot! Do you want to get us both fired?" ✩

BEHIND THE PUNCH LINE:
Improvisations

An *improvisation* is a comedy routine made up on the spot. A group of actors performing "improv," as it is known, often ask the audience for suggestions on the subjects of their routines, and then structure the comedy around whatever topic the audience gives them. For example, a member of the group might yell out to the audience, "We need a subject for a talk show!" Someone in the audience might yell back, "Broccoli addiction support group!" The actors will then pretend that they are on TV talking about their issues with broccoli. Improv is fun for the audience, too, because it makes them feel like they are part of the show.

Improvisation gives actors a chance to develop their comedy "chops." They need the fast pace of this technique to keep them on their toes. *Saturday Night Live* is based on improvisation, although the actors have scripted notes and cue cards to help them out at times.

It takes a lot of skill to keep a joke going for a long time and still make it funny. If you lose your audience, the routine loses its energy.

Most colleges and universities have improv groups for students, and there are a few professional troupes as well. Some of the most famous improv troupes include the Groundlings in Los Angeles, the Second City in Chicago, and the Upright Citizens Brigade in New York, all of which have seen more than a few actors go on to become stars.

There was a man who was born on the fifth day of the fifth month of 1955, whose lucky number was five. On his birthday he went to the racetrack and was astounded to see that in the fifth race (scheduled for five o'clock) a horse called Pentagram was running, with the odds of 55 to 1. Rushing off to the bank, the man was astonished to find he had $5,555.55 in his bank account. He withdrew the whole amount, dashed back to the races and bet all of it on Pentagram to win. Pentagram, obviously, came in fifth. ☆

What do you get when you cross a parrot with a pig?

A bird who hogs the conversation.

A man went to visit a friend and was amazed to find him playing cards with his dog. He watched the game in amazement for a while. "I can hardly believe my eyes!" he exclaimed. "That's the smartest dog I've ever seen."

"Nah, he's not so smart—he has a tell," the friend replied. "Every time he gets a good hand, he wags his tail." ☆

What do you get when you cross a dog with an omelet?

Pooched eggs.

mini SPOTLIGHT

Full House

Full House is the story of Danny Tanner, a San Francisco broadcaster whose wife has died in a car accident, leaving him the single father of three young girls, D. J., Stephanie, and Michelle. Rather than raise them alone, Danny enlists the help of his wife's brother, Jesse, an Elvis-impersonating, rock 'n' roll–loving musician, and his friend Joey, a stand-up comedian who specializes in silly voices. Kimmy Gibbler, the Tanners' over-the-top, talkative neighbor and D. J.'s best friend, is the goofiest character on the show. *Full House*'s comedic genius lies in the humor taken from everyday situations.

What do you get when you cross a sprinter with a dog?

The 100-yard Dachshund.

What do you get when you cross a dog with a journalist?

A Rover reporting.

What's better than a talking dog?

A spelling bee.

Why did the Doberman marry the Golden Retriever?

He found her very fetching.

What do you get when you cross a dog with a soldier?

A pooper trooper.

One day, a busy butcher notices a dog in his shop and shoos it away. Later, he finds the dog has come back, and the butcher sees that the dog has a note in its mouth, which reads: "Can I have 12 sausages and a leg of lamb, please." The butcher looks, and lo and behold, there's a $10 bill in the dog's mouth. So the butcher takes the money, puts the sausages and lamb in a bag, and places the bag in the dog's mouth. The butcher is very impressed, and since it's closing time, he decides to close up shop and see where the dog goes.

The dog walks down the street and comes to a crosswalk. It puts down the bag, jumps up, and presses the crossing button. Then it waits patiently, bag in mouth, for the light to change. The dog walks across the road with the butcher following. The dog then comes to a bus stop, and starts looking at the timetable. The butcher is in awe. The dog checks out the bus times, and sits on one of the seats to wait. Along comes a bus. The dog walks to the front of the bus, looks at the number, and goes back to its seat.

Another bus comes. Again the dog goes and looks at the number. It sees that it's the right bus, and climbs on. The butcher, by now completely flabbergasted, follows the dog onto the bus. The bus travels through town and out to the suburbs. Eventually the dog gets up, moves to the front of the bus, and, standing on its hind legs, rings the bell to stop the bus. The dog gets off, the groceries still in its mouth, and the butcher continues to follow it.

They walk down the road, and the dog approaches a house. It walks up the path, and drops the groceries on the step. Then it walks back down the path, takes a big run, and throws itself—whap!—against the door. It goes back down the path, takes another run, and throws itself—whap!—against the door again! There's no answer at the door, so the dog goes back down the path, jumps up on a narrow wall, and walks along the perimeter of the garden. It gets to a window, and bangs its head against it several times. It walks back, jumps off the wall, and waits at the door. The butcher watches as a big guy opens the door and starts yelling at the dog. The butcher runs up and stops the guy. "What are you doing? This dog is a genius. It could be on TV, for Pete's sake!" "Genius, my eye," the man says. "This is the second time this week he's forgotten his key!" ☆

What do you get when you cross a bear with a skunk?

Winnie the Pee-yew!

BEHIND THE PUNCH LINE:
Shaggy-Dog Jokes

Shaggy-dog jokes are those overly long and annoying stories that make you groan because they're full of meaningless details and absurd characters. In fact, most of the story has very little relation to the punch line. A good storyteller, though, can have people in stitches because the ending is often so stupid and unexpected. Shaggy-dog jokes get their name from an old long and pointless joke which was about a shaggy dog. Today, however, the stories can be about anything, as long as they are ridiculous and lengthy and told in a misleading way.

The Original Shaggy Dog? You Be the Judge

And now, for (a variation on) the original shaggy-dog story:

A man was reading his newspaper one morning at breakfast. Halfway through it, he noticed a large ad set in bold type. It promised $5,000 to whoever could find the advertiser's lost "shaggy dog" and return it to him in Timbuktu. The man didn't pay much attention to it. Later that day, however, the man found a dog running down the street that matched the description in the newspaper. It was a large shaggy sheepdog, and it did in fact look a bit lost. So the man put it on a leash. He bought a plane ticket for himself and the dog, and flew all the way to Timbuktu. He found the address that had been advertised in the paper and rang the doorbell. An older man answered the door.

"Look, sir," the man with the dog said, "I've found your dog."

"My dog was shaggy," the man replied, "but not quite that shaggy."

A wealthy businessman takes a trip to Asia and brings along his pet beagle. One day, the beagle decides to explore this new land and eventually finds himself lost. Wandering about, he notices a tiger heading quickly in his direction with the intent of having the beagle as a snack.

Worried, the beagle thinks, "Oh no, what am I going to do?" Just then he notices some bones on the ground close by, and being as clever as he is, he immediately settles down to chew on the bones with his back to the approaching cat.

Just as the tiger is about to pounce, the beagle says loudly, "Boy, that was one delicious tiger. I wonder if I can find another."

Hearing this, the tiger stops himself and slinks away, terrified, into the trees.

"Whew," says the tiger. "That was close. That beagle nearly had me."

Meanwhile, a monkey who was watching the whole scene from a nearby tree figures he can put this knowledge to good use and trade it for protection from the tiger. So he scurries off to go inform him. But the beagle sees the monkey heading after the tiger with great speed and figures that something must be up.

The monkey soon catches up with the tiger, spills the beans, and strikes a deal. The tiger is furious at being made a fool of and says, "Here, monkey, come along and see what I'm going to do to that conniving canine."

Now the beagle sees the tiger coming with the monkey and thinks, "What am I going to do now?" But instead of running, the clever beagle sits down with his back to his attackers, pretending he hasn't seen them yet. Just when they get close enough to hear, the beagle says: "Where's that darn monkey? I sent him off a while ago to bring me another tiger." ☆

A professional duck hunter is in the market for a new bird dog. His search ends when he finds a dog that can actually walk on water to retrieve a duck. Shocked by his find, the hunter is sure none of his friends will ever believe him. First, he decides to try to tell one of his friends, an eternal pessimist who refuses to be impressed by anything.

So the man invites his friend to hunt with him and his new dog. As they wait by the shore, a few ducks fly by. They shoot, and a duck falls. The dog responds and jumps into the water. But the dog does not sink. Instead, he walks across the water to retrieve the bird, never getting more than his paws wet. This continues all day long; each time a duck falls, the dog walks across the water to retrieve it.

The pessimist watches carefully, sees everything, but does not say a single word. On the drive home the hunter asks his friend, "Did you notice anything unusual about my new dog?"

"I sure did," replies his friend. "He can't swim." ☆

What happened to the cat when she swallowed a ball of wool?
She had mittens.

How do you make a puppy disappear?
Use Spot remover.

A dog with a bandaged foot limped into town one day. The sheriff approached the stranger and said: "What brings you to Dawson City?" The dog replied: "I'm looking for the man who shot my paw." ☆

What do you get when you put a kitten in a Xerox machine?
A copycat.

ha-ha-ha!

An out-of-towner drove his car into a ditch in a remote area in the country. Luckily, a local farmer came to help with her big, strong horse named Buddy. She hitched Buddy up to the car and yelled, "Pull, Nellie, pull!" Buddy didn't move. Then the farmer hollered, "Pull, Buster, pull!" Buddy didn't budge. Once more the farmer commanded, "Pull, Coco, pull!" Nothing. Then the farmer casually said, "Pull, Buddy, pull!" and the horse easily dragged the car out of the ditch. The motorist was most grateful and very curious. He asked the farmer why she had called her horse by the wrong name three times. The farmer said, "Oh, Buddy is blind, and if he thought he was the only one pulling, he wouldn't even try!" ☆

What do cats call mice?

Delicious.

Why did the cat family move next door to the mouse family?

So they could have the neighbors for dinner.

What do you get when you put your kitten in the refrigerator?

The coolest cat in town.

What's a cat's favorite color?

Purrrrrple.

Bert has announced that he's given up on trying to teach Kitty to come when he calls. He said he's moved on to something much easier—teaching dogs to climb trees. ☆

Down, Boy, Down!

21

What do you call a pooch who wakes up too early in the morning?

A groggy doggie.

What do you do with a broken dog?

Get him fixed.

What do you get from an Alaskan cow?

Ice cream.

What's fast, furry, and goes "foow, foow"?

A dog chasing a car that's in reverse.

Where can you leave your dog while you shop?

In the barking lot.

What do cats drink on hot summer afternoons?

Miced tea.

What do you get when you cross a leopard with a dishwasher?

Spots on your dishes.

Why won't banks allow kangaroos to open accounts?

Their checks always bounce.

A lion had to appear at the courthouse to prove he had been a good ruler of the animal kingdom. He was nervous about his first day in court, but his friends told him he'd be all right if he just focused on the questions the judge asked and answered them as best he could.

The lion dressed up in his very best suit, and got to court right on time. He smiled at the judge and was very polite. He was a little shocked when the judge asked him, "Are you a lion?"

"No, madam," stammered the lion. "I swear, I'm telling the truth!" ☆

A wildcat committed a horrible murder and then left the country. The police came upon the scene of the crime and were stumped. They found the paw prints and the broken lock, but were unable to catch the crook. How come?

They couldn't find the missing lynx. ☆

What do you call a grizzly bear with no teeth?

A gummy bear.

What do bears wear in their hair?

Bearettes.

What did the mother buffalo say to her son before he left?

"Bison."

23

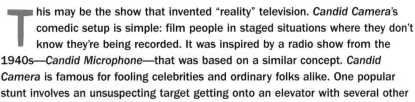

Candid Camera

This may be the show that invented "reality" television. *Candid Camera's* comedic setup is simple: film people in staged situations where they don't know they're being recorded. It was inspired by a radio show from the 1940s—*Candid Microphone*—that was based on a similar concept. *Candid Camera* is famous for fooling celebrities and ordinary folks alike. One popular stunt involves an unsuspecting target getting onto an elevator with several other riders (*Candid Camera* actors). When these riders enter, they don't turn and face the doors but instead face the back wall of the elevator. In time, the peer pressure gets to the target, and he or she turns around, too! Smile, you're on *Candid Camera*.

What did the mother kangaroo say when her baby was kidnapped?

"Somebody help me catch that pickpocket!"

A group of highway maintenance workers was sent to repair the road signs that some vandals had knocked over along a forested area. The first one they put back up was a MOOSE CROSSING sign.

As the workers moved to repair the next sign, one crew member looked back and spotted a moose running across the highway at the place they had just left. Turning to a coworker he said, "I wonder how long he's been waiting to cross?" ☆

> **Knock, knock.**
> *Who's there?*
> **Who.**
> *Who who?*
> **I didn't know you were an owl!**

Peter Rabbit was a very bad bunny. He never finished his carrots at dinner. He always hopped fences. And every day, he would sneak into a farmer's field and steal a head of lettuce. Every day for three weeks in a row, the farmer checked his garden and found a big hole where a lettuce head used to be.

One night the farmer decided he would catch the culprit, so he hid in some bushes by the garden. At sunrise, the farmer saw Peter sneak into the vegetables and chew off a head of lettuce. He jumped out from his hiding place and ran after Peter Rabbit. They ran through fields and through dales and across miles and miles of meadows. At the end of a long and exhausting chase, the angry farmer cornered Peter in a pumpkin patch. Why did he let him go?

For Pete's sake. ☆

Boy: Why didn't you pull a rabbit out of your hat?
Magician: Because I just washed my hare and
I can't get it to do anything now!

What do rabbits sing to each other once a year?
"Hoppy Birthday."

What do you get when you cross a cow with a volcano?
Udder disaster.

Why couldn't Noah catch many fish while he was on the Ark?
Because he had only two worms!

Why were all the mice in disguise?
They were attending a mousequerade party.

Why can't you play cards in the jungle?
Because of the cheetahs.

What do you call it when a bull swallows a stick of dynamite?
A-bomb-in-a-bull.

25

Please pass the antacid...

How does a mouse feel after it takes a bath?

Squeaky clean.

What's a mouse's least favorite sound?

The hiss of death.

Where do baby calves go for lunch?

The calf-eteria.

Why wouldn't the girl mouse move in with the boy mouse?

Because his house was such a hole in the wall.

What do you get when you cross a porcupine with a baby goat?

One stuck-up kid!

A woman opens her front door one morning to find a snail sitting on her doorstep. She swings her leg back and kicks the snail all the way down the walkway in front of her house. Two years later, the doorbell rings. When the woman answers the door, she looks down and there is the snail, who asks, "What was *that* all about?" ☆

Why did the farmer give the horse a hammer at bedtime?

Because he wanted the horse to hit the hay.

What goes trot-dash-trot-dash-dash?

Horse code.

Why do zebras have black and white stripes?

So they can referee football games.

What's the best way to stop a rhinoceros from jumping up and down on the bed?

What kind of horse makes you wake up scared?

A nightmare.

Why don't rabbits have black and white stripes?

Why on earth would a rabbit want to referee a football game?

Why did the chimp sell his banana store?

He was tired of all the monkey business.

Why wouldn't the pet store take back the chimp?

They didn't offer a monkey-back guarantee.

What dog loves to have its fur washed?

A shampoodle.

What do you call a crate of ducks?

A box of quackers.

Did you ever wonder if . . .

. . . milk comes out of a cow's nose when it laughs?

Put Krazy Glue on the ceiling.

What does a Dalmatian say after eating a particularly savory bowl of dog food?

"Oh yeah, that definitely hits the spots."

What's the easiest way to count a herd of cattle?

Use a cow-culator.

A camel, a giraffe, a donkey, and a pig all went to an audition at a comedy club. The camel went on first. He did an impersonation of a llama, told ten jokes, and then left the stage. The judges all laughed. Then the giraffe came out. First the giraffe cleared her throat, which took a little while. Then the giraffe did a headstand and told a few tall tales. The judges found her so funny that they asked her to come back the next day. The donkey went on stage next. The donkey had a really zany act, and the judges got a kick out of it. Finally, the pig stood at the microphone. He told a really, really, really, long shaggy-dog story about a circus dog. The joke was so long that it took the pig two hours to tell it. The judges were so upset that they threw the pig out of the club.

Why didn't the judges like the pig?

The pig was a real boar. ☆

What should you do when you're serving a camel tea?

Ask him if he'd like one hump or two.

What do you call a really good camel joke?

A hump-dinger.

A woman walks into a bar with a giraffe. The woman goes over to the bar to order a drink while the giraffe lies down. The bartender says to the woman, "Hey, you can't leave that lyin' on the floor!" The woman answers, "It's not a lion." ☆

HAI-BAAA!

What do you get when you cross a sheep with a kung fu master?

Lamb chops.

Why do kings have royal seals?

Because royal walruses eat too much.

What did the sheep say to his fiancée?

"There's something I have to tell you: I love ewe."

What do you call a sheep farm with only rams?

Ewes-less.

How do you toast a sheep?

"Here's to ewe."

Where did the sheep go after high school?

Ewe-niversity.

What do you call a lamb who does aerobics?

Sheep shape.

When is a sheep like a dog?

When it has fleece.

What do pigs see when they go to the ballet?

Swine Lake.

Why are pigs always in fashion?

They're sty-lish.

36

SIS-BOOM-BAA-BAA

How do sheep cheer for their favorite football team?

What do you call a go-go-dancing pig?

Shakin' bacon.

What did the pig say when he fell down the stairs?

"Oh, my achin' bacon."

What happened when the pig couldn't get up from his fall?

He called a ham-bulance.

A woman takes her hamster to the vet, and after a quick look at the creature, the vet pronounces it dead. Not happy with the vet's declaration, the woman asks for a second opinion. The vet gives a whistle and in comes a Labrador retriever. The dog sniffs at the hamster and pokes it a couple of times before shaking his head.

"Just as I thought," says the vet, "your hamster is dead." Still not happy, the woman asks for a third opinion. The vet opens the back door and in bounds a gray tabby. The cat jumps onto the table and looks the hamster up and down and nudges it with her paw for a few minutes before looking up and shaking her head.

"Yes, your hamster is definitely dead ma'am," says the vet. Finally convinced, the woman asks how much she owes.

"That will be $500, please," the vet answers.

"You are charging $500 just to tell me my hamster is dead?" says the woman, bewildered.

"Well," says the vet, "there's my prognosis, the lab report, and the cat scan." ☆

31

Where did the pig go to recover from his fall?

The hog-spital.

Which skunk lives in a church?

Pepe le Pew.

What kind of books do skunks read?

Best-smellers.

What do you call a teddy who wears flannel and cuts down trees for a living?

A lum-bear-jack.

What does the cow like to do on her day off?

Go to the moovies.

How do you play leapfrog with a hedgehog?

Very carefully.

TOMMY: I lost my dog yesterday.

SARAH: Oh no! Why don't you put an ad in the paper?

TOMMY: Don't be silly—he can't read!

CRITTER JITTERS

Creepy, Crawly, Slimy, Slithery Things

A tourist was fishing off the coast of Florida when his boat tipped over. He could swim, but he was afraid of alligators and hung on to the side of the overturned boat. Spotting an old beachcomber standing on the shore, the tourist shouted out, "Are there any 'gators around here?"

"Naw," the man hollered back. "They haven't been around here for years!"

Feeling safe, the tourist started swimming calmly toward the shore. About halfway there, he asked the guy, "How'd you get rid of the 'gators?"

"We didn't do anything," said the beachcomber. "The sharks got 'em." ✿

NO GATORS

ha-ha!

What do you call a mouse who hangs out with a bunch of pythons?

Lunch.

What do you get when you cross a parrot with a woodpecker?

A bird that talks in Morse code.

A woman goes into the local pet shop and asks the owner for a pet that can do everything. The owner thinks about it and says, "How about a dog?"

The woman replies, "No, I had a dog before. He was great but all he did was eat, sleep, and play fetch. I want a pet that can do everything!"

The owner thinks some more and says, "How about a cat?"

The woman replies, "No way! A cat certainly can't do everything; in fact, I've never seen them do anything! I want a pet that can do everything!"

The owner thinks for a long time and then says, "I've got it! What you want is a millipede!"

The woman looks at the owner skeptically and says, "A millipede? I can't imagine a millipede doing everything. But okay, I'll try a millipede."

When the woman gets the millipede home, she's eager to try him out, so she says to him, "Please clean the kitchen." Thirty minutes later, she walks into the

Did you hear about the caterpillar's stress attack?

kitchen and it's spotless. All the dishes are cleaned and neatly put away. The cabinets are clean and the floor is waxed. She's absolutely amazed.

Wanting to see what else he can do, the woman says to the millipede, "Please clean the living room." Twenty-five minutes later, she walks into the living room, and again everything's perfect. The carpets have been vacuumed. The furniture is cleaned and dusted. The woman is once again impressed.

The woman thinks to herself, "This is the most amazing thing I've ever seen. This pet really can do everything." Wanting him to do more, she says to the millipede, "Run down to the corner store and get me a newspaper, please." The millipede walks out of the living room.

Ten minutes go by and no millipede. Twenty minutes go by and still no millipede. After thirty minutes the woman is starting to wonder what's going on. It should have taken the millipede only a couple of minutes. But forty-five minutes later and still no millipede.

Deciding to look for him, the woman goes to leave out the front door. She opens the door and the millipede is just sitting on the front steps. The woman becomes furious. She says, "Hey! Where have you been all this time? I asked you 45 minutes ago to go to the corner store and get me a newspaper. Then I come to find you and you're sitting down on the job. What's going on?"

The millipede replies, "I'm going. I just have to put my shoes on!" ✩

He totally bugged out.

What did the fly say to the flypaper?

"I'm stuck on you."

JACK: Say, Jill, how did you get a swollen nose?

JILL: I bent down to smell a brose in my garden.

JACK: Not brose; it's rose, Jill. There's no *B* in rose.

JILL: There was in this one!

A snail goes into a car dealership. She asks the salesperson if they sell red convertibles. The salesperson answers, "Yes. But do you have a proper license, and the money to pay for the car?" The snail replies, "Yes, I've got both. The thing is, I'll only buy the car on one condition—that you have a big S painted on the sides of the car." The salesperson thinks about that for a moment. It seems odd to him, but it isn't every day that he sells an expensive convertible, so he agrees.

A few weeks later, the car is all ready and the salesperson calls the snail to tell her she can come pick it up. The snail is really pleased with her car and thanks him. The salesperson is still wondering about the reason for the big S on the car and asks, "So why did you want an S painted on the sides of the car?"

The snail replies, "When I drive by, I want everyone to say, 'Look at that S car go!'" ☆

ZZZZT!

If only you knew the power of the DARK SIDE!

What do you get when you cross a centipede and a parrot?

A walkie-talkie.

What do you get when you cross a Jedi knight with a toad?

Star Warts.

Monty Python's Flying Circus

Good day, hello, and welcome to the Monty Python's Flying Circus spotlight! Don't know who these chaps are? Monty Python is a group of British sketch comedians known for their serious silliness. The Pythons, as they are sometimes called, were the creators and stars of *Monty Python's Flying Circus,* a TV comedy series that ran from 1969 to 1974. The troupe was composed of Graham Chapman, John Cleese, Eric Idle, Terry Jones, Michael Palin, and Terry Gilliam. Gilliam, the one American in the troupe, was the man behind the absurd cartoons featured in each episode.

Memorable sketches included "The Argument Sketch," where a man pays to have an argument, and "The Dead Parrot Sketch," where an angry customer tries to get a refund from a pet-store owner who sold him a dead bird. The Pythons are known for continually cross-dressing and for finding the absurd in everyday situations. They even treated issues such as politics, the class system, and racism in a silly fashion, bringing serious topics onto mainstream television in a funny way in order to make their point.

The Pythons are also known for their theater tours, computer games, music recordings—even a Broadway musical! Python films made it to the box office, including *Monty Python and the Holy Grail* (1975), *The Life of Brian* (1979), and *The Meaning of Life* (1983). Right! Enough of this silliness! In the words of the Python's trademark line (which was also the title of a 1971 film), "And now for something completely different!"

BABY SNAKE: Mom, are we poisonous?
MOM SNAKE: We most certainly are!
BABY SNAKE: Are you *sure* we're poisonous?
MOM SNAKE: Yes, we are the most poisonous snake in the world. Why?
BABY SNAKE: I just bit my lip!

Two ants wandered into a large-screen TV. After crawling around for hours and hours the first ant started to cry. "I think we're lost! We'll never get out!"

"Don't worry," said the second ant. "I brought along a TV guide." ☆

What does a reptile wear on its feet?
Snakers.

Why couldn't the frog find his car?
It got toad away.

What's the strongest insect in the world?
A snail. It carries its house on its back!

How does a bee get to school?
It takes the buzz.

PRACTICAL JOKE

Want to really gross out your classmates? Tell them you've eaten *dudu.*

After they recover from the shock, tell them it's an African specialty made of fried, salted *bugs:* ants, bees, crickets, and cicadas. Mmm, tasty!

What do you call an insect that goes "Buzz-mzz-ummz-mzz"?
A mumble bee.

A snail is mugged by three turtles, but when the police ask the snail to give a description of what happened, all he can say is, "I don't know, officer. It all happened so fast!" ☆

Why do bees buzz?

Because they can't whistle.

39

THE MAKING OF A COMEDIAN
Step 2: Rehearsing

Although many comedy routines sound as though they were made up on the spur of the moment, every good comedian spends a great deal of time rehearsing. Even improv comedians have to practice! Rehearsal helps you make your routine smooth. You need to practice your pacing: when to pause, what to emphasize. You need to set the right tone: cheerful, somber, sarcastic.

Think of yourself as a joke samurai. A samurai is a Japanese warrior whose code of conduct forbids showing any sign of weakness before others. A good joke samurai should never let the audience see his or her weakness.

Every professional comedian has spent time practicing the art of joke telling, and has studied his or her punch lines really well. Just remember, if an audience thinks that you don't know what you're doing, they'll be too uncomfortable to laugh even if you've said something hilarious. Ask an adult to explain any of the material in this book that you don't understand before you go out and dazzle your friends.

A man was driving down a lonely country road when it began to snow heavily. His windows fogged up, and his wiper blades were badly worn and soon fell apart. The man couldn't see out of the front of his car anymore and he couldn't continue to drive, so he stopped the car. Then he got out and started to turn over large rocks. Finally, he found two frozen snakes. He straightened them out and stuck them flat onto his wiper blades, and they worked just fine. Haven't you ever heard of "wind-chilled vipers"? ☆

Why doesn't a python use silverware?

Because he has a forked tongue.

Once upon a time in a magical land, there lived a snake named Nate. In this land, actually rather close to Nate's house, there was a great road, and next to this road was a lever. The lever was ancient, and the myth around the lever was that if you were to push it, it would trigger the end of the world. One day, Nate was slithering down the road. When he came upon the lever, he began crossing the road so he could get a look at it. At the same moment, a truck came zooming around the corner, and the driver found himself in a dilemma: either hit the snake and run him over, or swerve, hit the lever, and end the world. Needless to say, the driver ran over Nate and went on his merry way. What's the moral of this story?

Better Nate than lever. ☆

What does a boa constrictor call his girlfriend?

A grasshopper walks into a bar and the bartender says, "We have a drink named after you." The grasshopper replies, "You have a drink named Albert?" ☆

A millipede ran into a centipede on the street. The millipede said in surprise, "Wow, what are the odds of this?!"

"Oh," answered the centipede, "about 10 to 1." ☆

What did the termite do when she couldn't carry the twig on her own?
She hired an assist-ant.

A frog is walking along one day when he comes across a fairy.

"For forty bucks," the fairy says, "I can turn you into a prince."

"Wow!" exclaims the frog, and gives the fairy fifty dollars.

The fairy changes the frog into a handsome, dashing prince. The former frog is overjoyed.

"It'll be so much easier to get a date for the ball now," he thinks.

So the prince asks the fairy for the ten bucks that was left over so he can rent a really snazzy limo to the next ball. The magic fairy gives him the money and is about to leave when suddenly the prince shrinks down in his boots, turns green, and is once again a frog. Shocked and despairing, the frog stares at the magic fairy. "What happened?" he asks.

"Well," she replies, "You gave me fifty bucks and then asked for your change back." ☆

His Main Squeeze!

41

What do you get when you cross kangaroos with geckos?

Leaping lizards!

What kind of lizard loves to tell jokes?

A silly-mander.

Why is it so hard to fool a snake?

Because you can't pull its leg.

Why did the bug family stay home on their last vacation?

The roach motel was full.

Why did the mama ladybug ground her kids?

They were bugging her.

What is a frog's favorite soda?

Croaka-Cola.

Some Boy Scouts from the city were on a camping trip. The mosquitoes were so fierce that the boys had to hide under their blankets to avoid getting bitten. Then one of them saw some lightning bugs and said to his friend, "We might as well give up. They're coming after us with flashlights." ✩

42

FOWL PLAY

Birds of a Feather Flock Together

What do you get when you mix a bird with a blender?
Shredded tweet.

What shape is like a lost parrot?
Polygon.

What do you call a bird that's been eaten by a cat?

A swallow.

What do you call the second bird that's been eaten by the same cat?
An after-dinner tweet.

One day a man walked into a bird shop carrying a beak. "I'm looking for a bird to match this beak," he said to the owner.

"No problem," said the owner. "I've got one that'll fit the bill." ☆

Why did the bird make fun of everyone?
It was a mockingbird!

ALEX: Did you hear the story about the peacock?
TRISH: No, but I heard it's a beautiful tale!

Why did the teacher send the duck to the principal's office?
He was making wisequacks.

How do baby birds know how to fly?
They just wing it.

Why did the bird sit on the fish?
The fish was a perch.

If a seagull flies over the sea, what flies over the bay?
A bagel.

What do you get when you cross a duck with a large reptile?
A quack-odile.

Is chicken soup good for your health?
Not if you're the chicken!

Who tells the best chicken jokes?
Comedi-hens.

Why did the duck become a spy?
He was good at quacking codes.

44

Hey, my allergy to feathers is gone!

Miranda Cosgrove

Miranda Cosgrove was discovered at the very young age of three. She was at a restaurant with her family, singing and dancing around the table, when she was approached by an agent. Soon, she was appearing in commercials for McDonald's and Burger King.

She then moved on to play minor roles in several television shows. It was her first movie role, as the know-it-all teacher's pet, Summer, in *School of Rock* (2003) with Jack Black, that really launched her career. The movie was a box office hit and helped her get her first major TV role, as the little sister on *Drake & Josh,* where her character made her TV brothers' lives as miserable as possible—in the most hilarious ways!

The show ended after three seasons, but her talent landed her the lead role in her own hysterical TV series, *iCarly*. Miranda even got to put her musical talents to use, performing the theme song to *iCarly* along with former TV big brother Drake Bell. And in 2008, she starred in the movie *iCarly: iGo to Japan*.

In addition to filming the show, she also lends her voice to animated movies. She was Margo in *Despicable Me* (2010) and its sequel (2013). Movies, TV, singing . . . What will she do next?

A lady goes into a pet store one day. "I'm really lonely," she says to the clerk. "I need a pet to keep me company."

"Well," replies the clerk, "how about this nice parrot? He'll talk to you."

"Hey, that's great," says the lady. She buys the parrot and takes him home. The next day the lady comes back to the pet store. "You know, that parrot isn't talking to me yet," she says.

"Hmm, let's see," says the clerk. "I know! You buy this little ladder for his cage. He'll climb the ladder, and then he'll talk." So off she goes with a newly purchased ladder. The next day she comes back again.

"Hey, that parrot still hasn't said a word," she says to the pet-store clerk.

He thinks a minute. "How about this little mirror?" he says. "You hang it at the top of the ladder. The parrot will climb the ladder, look in the mirror, and then he'll talk to you."

"Okay," she says, and buys the little mirror and goes home. But the next day that same lady is back in the shop. "Well, I'm getting a bit discouraged," she says. "That parrot *still* won't talk to me."

The clerk scratches his head. "Let me think. Aha! Try this bell. You hang it over the mirror. The parrot will climb the ladder, look in the mirror, ring the bell, and then he will surely talk to you!"

I need a new mirror— this one is getting blurry...

"All right, I'll give it a try," says the lady. And she buys the bell and takes it home. The next day the same lady comes back to the pet shop, and she is very distressed.

"What's wrong?" asks the clerk.

"My parrot . . . well, he died," she answers quietly.

"Oh my gosh! I'm so sorry for your loss!" exclaims the clerk. "But I have to ask you, did the parrot ever say anything to you?"

"Oh yes, he said one thing, right before he died," she replies.

"Well, what did he say?" asks the clerk.

The lady replies, "He said, 'Doesn't that store carry any food?'" ☆

Why was the bird arrested?

He was a robin.

47

Why did the rooster cross the road?

To show he wasn't a chicken.

ha-ha!

A duck walks into a drugstore and asks for a tube of lipstick. The cashier says, "That'll be $1.49," and the duck replies, "Just put it on my bill." ☆

What should you do when someone throws a goose at you?

Duck.

What do you say when someone throws a duck at a duck?

"Duck, duck!"

What do you say when someone throws a goose at a duck?

"Duck, duck, goose!"

A magician has been working on a cruise ship doing the same act for many years. The audiences like him, and they change often enough that he doesn't have to worry about finding new tricks. But the captain's parrot sits in the back row and watches him night after night, year after year. After a while, the parrot figures out how the tricks work and starts giving the secrets away to the audiences. When the magician makes a bouquet of flowers disappear, for instance, the parrot squawks, "Behind his back! Behind his back!" Well, the magician gets really annoyed at this, but he doesn't know what to do, since the parrot belongs to the captain. One day, the ship springs a leak and sinks. The magician manages to grab hold of a plank of wood and floats on it. The parrot flies over and sits on the other end. They drift and drift for three days without speaking. On the morning of the fourth day, the parrot looks over at the magician and says, "Okay, I give up. Where did you hide the ship?" ✩

It's in the hat, smart guy!

Why wouldn't anybody go to the duck doctor?

They all knew he was a quack.

Why can't you play hide-and-seek with poultry in a Chinese restaurant?

Because of the Peking duck.

What's orange and sounds like a parrot?

A carrot.

BEHIND THE PUNCH LINE:
Slapstick

Slapstick comedy is just the opposite of stand-up comedy. It's comedy where the comedian doesn't stand up, but falls down! The name "slapstick" comes from a kind of wooden stick used by clowns to hit each other on stage. The slapstick was split down the middle and designed to make a very loud, funny, slapping noise without inflicting any damage on the recipient of the blow. During the nineteenth century, a little bit of gunpowder was plugged into the crack in the stick to make the slaps even more explosive.

Slapstick comedy is very physical and it's hard work. Whether he's getting slapped in the face, poked in the eye, or hit with a pie, the slapstick comic is the victim—or perpetrator—of an endless series of gags and practical jokes. Jim Carrey is an excellent example of a slapstick comedian. He makes faces, contorts his body, and does stunts and pratfalls (a staged fall — carefully done so the comedian doesn't get hurt), all in the name of comedy.

What has wings, feathers, and fangs?

Count Duckula.

Why did the chicken cross the road?

To get the New York Times.
Get it?
No.
Neither do I. I get USA Today.

What do you get when a chicken lays eggs on top of a hill?

Eggrolls.

49

Why did the chicken cross the road?
She thought it would be egg-citing.

Why did the chicken cross the playground?
To get to the other slide.

Why did the chicken cross the ocean?
To get to the other tide.

Why did the chicken cross the amusement park?
To get to the other ride.

Why did the chicken cross the basketball court?
He heard the referee calling fouls.

Why did the daredevil cross the road?
She wanted to play chicken.

THE WORLD'S OLDEST JOKE:

Why did the chicken cross the road?

To get to the other side.

50

Why did the turkey cross the road?

Why did the chicken bounce across the road?
It was a rubber chicken.

Why did the rubber chicken cross the road?
She wanted to stretch her legs.

Why did the muddy chicken cross the road and then cross back?
He was a dirty double-crosser.

Akemi got a parrot for her birthday. This parrot was fully grown, with a bad attitude and an even worse vocabulary. Every other word was naughty or rude. Akemi tried very hard to change the bird's manners. She would always say polite words, play soft music, anything she could think of to try to set a good example, but nothing worked. Akemi was getting really frustrated. She yelled at the bird, and the bird got worse. She shook the bird, and the bird got angrier and ruder. One day, Akemi felt so desperate that she put the parrot in the freezer. For a few moments she heard the bird squawking, kicking, and screaming, and then suddenly everything was quiet. She was frightened that she might have hurt the bird and quickly opened the freezer door. The parrot calmly stepped out on to her arm and said: "I'm sorry that I might have offended you with my language and actions and I ask for your forgiveness. I will try to correct my behavior." Akemi was amazed at the great change in the bird and was about to ask what had caused it when the parrot continued: "May I ask what the chicken did?" ☆

51

What did they call the canary that flew into the dessert?

Tweety pie.

Three birds walk into a bar. The fourth one ducks. ☆

Why is it easy for chicks to talk?

Because talk is cheep.

What do you call it when a chicken stumbles as it crosses the street?

A road trip.

How do birds dance?

Chick to chick.

The chicken was on strike.

SPOTLIGHT

Mindy Kaling

Named after one of the title characters of the classic TV sitcom *Mork and Mindy*, Mindy Kaling (born Vera Mindy Chokalingam) was clearly destined for comedy. Inspired by the only American show on TV in Nigeria at the time she was pregnant, and having already decided to move to the States, Mindy's mother wanted Mindy to have a cute American name.

While attending Dartmouth College, Kaling practiced her comedic timing with the improvisational comedy troupe the Dog Day Players. She also created the comic strip *Badly Drawn Girl*, which was featured in the *Dartmouth* (the college's daily newspaper), and was a writer for the Dartmouth *Jack-O-Lantern* (the college's humor magazine).

In 2003, after graduating, she portrayed Ben Affleck in a play titled *Matt & Ben*, which she cowrote with her friend Brenda Withers. The play was named one of *Time* magazine's "Top Ten Theatrical Events of the Year." The play helped her land her most recognizable role, as the superficial, seemingly dim-witted Kelly Kapoor on NBC's hit show *The Office*. Not only did she star in the show, but she also wrote some of its episodes and was a coexecutive producer.

Mindy's film career is also on the rise and she has appeared in a few blockbuster hits. Her first movie role was in *Office* castmate Steve Carell's *The 40-Year-Old Virgin* (2005). She also appeared in the 2011 romantic comedy *No Strings Attached* with Natalie Portman and Ashton Kutcher, as well as the 2012 comedy *The Five-Year Engagement* with Jason Segel. And in 2012, Mindy developed her own television show, *The Mindy Project,* which she stars in, writes, and produces.

As a writer, producer, and actor, it is clear that Mindy can truly do it all.

What do you get when you cross a chicken with chewing gum?

Chicklets.

ROOSTER: Wow, did you hear the voice on that little chick?
HEN: That's what you call beginner's cluck.

What do chickens do when they're in love?

They give each other pecks.

Why was the chicken team so bad at baseball?

They kept hitting fowl balls.

Why was the little boy afraid of the turkey?

He heard it was a gobblin'.

Why didn't the turkey finish his dinner?

He was already stuffed.

What do you get when you put a bird in the freezer?

A brrrd.

A police officer sees a man driving by with a bunch of penguins in the backseat. The officer pulls the man over and asks, "Where did you get those penguins?"

The man replies, "I found them wandering on the side of the road."

"Well, you should take them to the zoo," the cop says.

The next day the police officer sees the same man drive by, with the penguins still in his backseat. Once again he pulls the car over, and he says, "I thought I told you to take those penguins to the zoo!"

"I did," the man replies. "Today, I'm taking them to the beach." ☆

CHICKLETS
WITH THAT GREAT FEATHERS-IN-YOUR-TEETH FLAVOR!

53

What did the owl do when she got fired?

Nothing. She didn't give a hoot.

Why do hummingbirds hum?

Because they don't know the words!

A little boy goes into a pet store and asks the store owner for some bird seed. The owner asks, "How many birds do you have?"

The boy replies, "None yet. I need the seeds to grow them!" ✩

What do you give a sick bird?
Tweetment.

Which bird is always out of breath?
The puffin.

What bird steals soap from the bathtub?

Robber ducks.

What's the name of the bestselling biography of 400 famous owls?

Who's Who.

Why wouldn't the canary pay for his date's dinner?

He was too cheep.

Why is a sofa like a roasted turkey?

Because they're both filled with stuffing.

54

SOUNDS FISHY TO ME

It'll Hook You Right Away

What do you call a Fish with no eye?

A Fsh.

What kind of hair does the ocean have?
Wavy.

What did the ocean say to the shore?
"Glad to sea you!"

Why do oceans never go out of style?
They're always current.

Why do fish swim in salt water?
Because pepper makes them sneeze!

Mike went fishing one day, but at the end he had not caught a single fish. On the way back home, he stopped at a fish store.

"I want to buy three trout, please," he said to the owner. "But instead of putting them in a bag, can you throw them to me?"

"Throw them? Why do you want me to do that?" the owner asked.

Mike replied, "So I can tell everyone that I caught three fish!" ☆

Why do fish like worms?

Because they're hooked on them.

When is fishing not a good way to relax?

When you're the worm.

56

Two goldfish are in a tank. One says to the other, "Do you know how to drive this thing?" ☆

Turn left at the bubbling treasure chest, soldier!

What kind of fish goes with peanut butter?

Jellyfish!

What day does a fish hate the most?

Fryday!

What do you get when you mix a fish and an elephant?

Swimming trunks.

Tina Fey

Tina Fey's incredible comedic career began with the improvisational comedy troupe the Second City in Chicago. It was there that she auditioned for the team behind *Saturday Night Live* and she was hired as a writer. Her success behind the scenes was so great that she went on to become the first-ever female head writer of *SNL*, eventually earning a starring role as the coanchor of the popular "Weekend Update" segment, first with Jimmy Fallon and later with Amy Poehler. What is probably her most famous role on *SNL* came years later, when she did a satirical impersonation of Republican vice-presidential candidate Sarah Palin.

In 2004, she adapted the screenplay *Mean Girls* from the nonfiction book *Queen Bees and Wannabes* by Rosalind Wiseman. Fey also starred in the smash hit as a quirky, wannabe-hip math teacher. In 2006,

she created the hit sitcom *30 Rock,* which is loosely based on her experiences behind the scenes at *SNL.* She would also go on to star in other movies, including *Baby Mama* (2008), where she plays a single businesswoman who discovers she can't get pregnant and enlists an unlikely choice (*SNL* costar Amy Poehler) to be her surrogate; and *Date Night* (2010), where she and costar Steve Carell play a couple pretending to be a different couple in order to have a glamorous night out, only to have the night turn into something more thrilling and dangerous. In 2015, she created the hit show *Unbreakable Kimmy Schmidt.*

Fey is a critically acclaimed writer and actress who has won several Emmy Awards, Golden Globe Awards, Screen Actors Guild Awards, and Writers Guild of America Awards. Though she considered herself a "supernerd" in high school and college, we consider her supertalented.

BEHIND THE PUNCH LINE:

Stand-Up Comedy

Imagine how much fun it would be to get paid just for being funny! Well, stand-up comics are professional comedians who do just that. *Stand-up comedy* is exactly what it sounds like—someone stands up in front of other people and tries to make them laugh. Stand-up comedians prepare a series of jokes, skits, and wisecracks for their routines. Often, they will also impersonate, or mimic, famous people. Comedians typically open a show with a monologue, a long solo speech. A monologue often consists of a string of jokes on one topic with no break in between. Most comedians perform in comedy clubs, which are theaters or nightclubs that hire comedians to entertain

58

What is a shark's favorite game?

Swallow the leader.

What do you call a fish's date?

His gill-friend.

What did the ocean say to the shore?

Nothing, it just waved.

What do you call a fish that can do magic?

Marlin the Magnificent.

Many years ago, a woman gave birth to twin sons. She and her husband, a fisherman, loved their children very much, but couldn't think of what to name them. Finally, after a few days, the husband said, "Let's not decide on names right now. If we wait a little while, the names will simply come to us."

After several weeks had passed, the couple noticed something peculiar. When left alone, one of the boys would always turn toward the sea, while the other boy would face inland. It didn't matter which way the parents positioned  the children, the same child always faced the same direction. "Let's call the boys Toward and Away," suggested the woman. Her husband agreed, and from that point on, the boys were known simply as Toward and Away.

The years passed and the lads grew tall and strong. The day came when the aging fisherman said to his sons, "Boys, it is time that you learn how to make a living from the sea." The three of them filled their ship with supplies, said their good-byes, and set sail for a three-month voyage. The three months passed quickly for the woman, yet the ship had not returned. Another three months passed, and still no ship.

Three whole years passed before the grieving woman saw a lone man walking toward her house. She recognized him as her husband. "My goodness! What has happened to my darling boys?" she cried. The ragged fisherman began to tell his story: "We were just barely one whole day out to sea when Toward hooked into a great fish. Toward fought long and hard, but the fish was more than his equal. For a whole week they wrestled upon the waves without either of them letting up. Yet eventually the great fish started to win the battle, and Toward was pulled over the side of our ship. He was swallowed whole, and we never saw either of them again."

"Oh dear, that must have been terrible! What a huge fish that must have been!" said the woman.

"Yes, it was, but you should have seen the one that got Away!" ☆

59

What do you call a boat's date?

Her buoy-friend.

A fish needed surgery, but didn't know if he'd be able to pay for it. He met with the doctor to talk about how much it would cost. "Don't worry at all," said the doctor. "I'll give you a discount on the price. I admire and respect your cousin, so I am honored to be taking care of his family. He is, beyond any doubt, an excellent sturgeon." ☆

Two friends decided to go on a fishing trip. They rented all the necessary equipment: the rods, the reels, the rowboat, the car, and even a cabin in the woods. They spent a fortune.

The first day they went fishing, they had no luck and didn't catch anything. The same thing happened on the next day, and the next. This continued each day until finally, on the last day of their vacation, one of the men caught a fish.

As they drove home, they became really depressed. One of the friends turned to the other and said, "Do you realize that catching this one lousy fish cost us almost a thousand dollars?"

The other friend replied, "Wow. I guess it's a good thing we didn't catch any more!" ☆

CLASSY JOKES
Classroom Distractions

TEACHER: James, do you use bad words?
JAMES: No, sir.
TEACHER: Do you disobey your parents?
JAMES: No, sir.
TEACHER: Come now, you must do something wrong every once in a while!
JAMES: I tell lies.

TEACHER: Mrs. Jones, I asked you to come in to discuss Johnny's appearance.
MRS. JONES: Why? What's wrong with his appearance?
TEACHER: He hasn't made one in this classroom since September.

This class is so hoisy I can't hear myself speak!

You aren't missing much...

PRACTICAL JOKES

Freak out your parents!

Tape the sprayer on your kitchen sink into the "on" position late at night. The first person to turn on the water in the morning will get soaked. (Just make sure it's not you!!!)

Scare the living daylights out of your little brother!

Take a picture of the creepiest, scariest, grossest monster you can find and hide it somewhere in your house. Lead your younger sibling to the hiding place, swear him to secrecy, then reveal the photo and say it's a photo of him when he was born.

Work your big sister into a lather!

Tell her that one of her friends called (for this to work, be specific—use the real name of someone your sibling is close to) and said one of the coolest kids at school is having a party tonight, but you can't remember all the details. Then run and hide for the rest of the day.

TEACHER: Amy, I've had to send you to the principal's office every day this week. What do you have to say for yourself?
AMY: I'm glad it's Friday!

PRINCIPAL: Esmé, did you really call your teacher a meanie?
ESMÉ: Yes, I did.
PRINCIPAL: And is it true you called her a wicked old witch?
ESMÉ: Yes, it is.
PRINCIPAL: And did you also call her a tomato-nosed beanbag?
ESMÉ: No, but I'll remember that for next time!

TEACHER: Sam, if I put a dozen marbles in my right pocket, fifteen marbles in my left pocket, and thirty-one marbles in my back pocket, what would I have?
SAM: Heavy pants!

TEACHER: Kevin, how do you spell *crocodile*?
KEVIN: K-R-O-K-O-D-I-A-L.
TEACHER: No, I'm sorry, that's wrong.
KEVIN: It can't be. You asked me how *I* spell it!

A tutor who tooted the flute
Tutored two tooters to toot.
Said the two to the tutor,
"Is it easier to toot or
To tutor two tooters to toot?"

Why do magicians do so well in school?

They're good at trick questions.

63

Why did the cyclops have to close his school?

Because he had only one pupil.

Why was the little bird suspended from school?

It was caught peeping.

A little girl was counting to ten for her math teacher.

"One, two, three, four, five," she said. "Six, seven, eight, ten!"

"Didn't you forget something?" prompted the teacher. "What happened to nine?"

"No," replied the girl. "Seven eight nine." ☆

How much fun can you have doing arithmetic?

Sum fun!

BOY: Isn't our principal stupid?
GIRL: Hey, do you know who I am?
BOY: No, why should I?
GIRL: I'm the principal's daughter.
BOY: Do you know who I am?
GIRL: No.
BOY: Thank goodness!

Why was the teacher cross-eyed?

Because he couldn't control his pupils!

Charlie Chaplin

Charlie Chaplin was born in London, England, in 1889. The son of two music-hall performers, he grew up around entertainers, and it's said that the first time he stepped on stage was when he was five, filling in for his mother when she was too sick to perform!

Chaplin immigrated to the United States in his early 20s, where he was soon picked up as an actor by the Keystone Film Company. He succeeded in the trademark silent films Keystone was producing—movies with no recorded soundtrack or dialogue— thanks to the famous "Tramp" character he developed. This persona was a homeless man who—despite his silly costume of a tight coat and oversize pants, shoes, and hat—had the proper manners of a gentleman.

As Chaplin proved his talent, he got more creative control over his comedy. In 1921, he released the film *The Kid*, which he produced and directed himself. Altogether, Chaplin produced more than 80 films and even earned a star on the Hollywood Walk of Fame for his comic genius.

Once, at the height of his popularity, he entered a Charlie Chaplin look-alike contest under a different name as a joke, and he finished in third place!

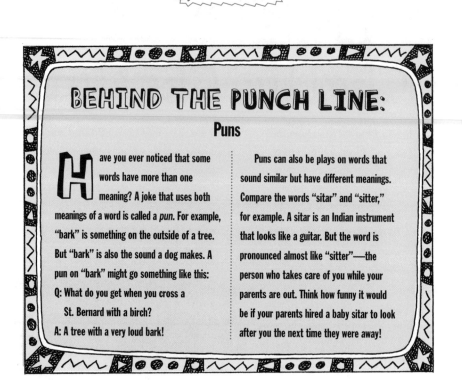

BEHIND THE PUNCH LINE:

Puns

Have you ever noticed that some words have more than one meaning? A joke that uses both meanings of a word is called a *pun*. For example, "bark" is something on the outside of a tree. But "bark" is also the sound a dog makes. A pun on "bark" might go something like this:

Q: What do you get when you cross a St. Bernard with a birch?

A: A tree with a very loud bark!

Puns can also be plays on words that sound similar but have different meanings. Compare the words "sitar" and "sitter," for example. A sitar is an Indian instrument that looks like a guitar. But the word is pronounced almost like "sitter"—the person who takes care of you while your parents are out. Think how funny it would be if your parents hired a baby sitar to look after you the next time they were away!

One by one, a class of fifth-graders were called on to make sentences with words chosen by their teacher. Nick didn't often participate in class, so his teacher was glad when she saw him raise his hand to give it a try.

"Nick," said the teacher, "make a sentence with the words 'defeat,' 'defense,' 'deduct,' and 'detail.'"

Nick thought for a few minutes and smiled. He shouted, "Defeat of deduct went over defense before detail!" ☆

How are a king and a yardstick alike?

They're both rulers.

CHEMISTRY TEACHER: What is the formula for water?
STUDENT: H-I-J-K-L-M-N-O.
CHEMISTRY TEACHER: Why would you give a silly answer like that?
STUDENT: You said it was H to O!

TEACHER: José, go to the map and find North America.
JOSÉ: Here it is!
TEACHER: Correct. Now, class, who discovered North America?
CLASS (in unison): José!

SAM: Would you punish me for something I didn't do?
TEACHER: No, of course not.
SAM: Good, because I didn't do my homework.

mini SPOTLIGHT

The Office

Based on the hit BBC series of the same name, *The Office* is a "mockumentary" of the everyday lives of Dunder Mifflin Paper Company employees. Most of the laughs surround the oblivious but well-intentioned boss, Michael Scott (Steve Carell). Under his leadership—and that of the bosses who followed, including Andy Bernard (Ed Helms) and Robert California (James Spader)—the employees often find their days of tedium interrupted by unnecessary field trips, useless meetings, office hijinks, crafty pranks, and anything else that will sidetrack work.

What do you call a student who can subtract, multiply, and divide but can't add?

A total failure.

TEACHER: Why were the early days of history called the Dark Ages?
TOMMY: Because there were so many knights.

Why did George Washington chop down the cherry tree?

I'm stumped.

Why was the math book sad?

It had too many problems.

TEACHER: What is half of 8?
LUCY: Up and down or across?
TEACHER: What do you mean?
LUCY: Well, up and down makes 3 and across makes 0.

What's the difference between teachers and trains?

Trains say "Choo Choo!" and teachers say "Spit that gum out!"

"Johnny," said the teacher, "please make up a sentence using the word 'lettuce.'"

Johnny thought a minute and said, "Please lettuce leave class early today!" ☆

Yoon came to school without her homework assignment.

"Where is your homework?" asked her teacher.

"I ate it," said Yoon.

"But why did you do such a thing?" asked her teacher.

"You told the class yesterday that it would be a piece of cake." ☆

What's the capital of California?

C.

TEACHER: What does the word *benign* mean?
SARA: Benign is what you will be after you be eight.

Why is animal testing a bad idea?

Because they get nervous and give all the wrong answers.

TEACHER: If I gave you four cats today and six cats tomorrow, how many cats would you have?
JANE: Eleven.
TEACHER: That's not right, you'd have ten.
JANE: No, Miss, I'd have eleven. I already have one cat at home!

On the first day of class, the teacher asked any troublemakers to stand up. After a few moments of silence, a shy little girl stood up. "Are you a troublemaker?" the teacher asked.

"No," replied the girl, "I just hate to see you standing there all by yourself." ☆

TEACHER: How old were you on your last birthday?
CHARLIE: Eight.
TEACHER: How old will you be on your next birthday?
CHARLIE: Ten.
TEACHER: That's impossible.
CHARLIE: No, it isn't. I'm nine today.

TEACHER: Why are you late?
DANA: Because of the sign.
TEACHER: What sign?
DANA: The one that says, "SCHOOL AHEAD, GO SLOW."

A frog expert from the aquarium gave a talk to a third-grade class. "It's easy to tell the male frogs from the female frogs," she said. "When you feed them, the male frogs will only eat female flies, and the female frogs will only eat male flies."

"But how do you know which flies are male and which are female?" asked a boy sitting at the back of the class.

"How am I supposed to know?" replied the woman. "I'm a frog expert." ☆

A speaker was booked to address an audience at a university. About two hours before she was supposed to speak, however, a couple of student jokers loaded all the folding chairs from the auditorium into a truck and drove off. No one knew about this until the audience began to arrive for the lecture. It was too late to do anything about it, and the audience had to stand throughout her talk. That evening she wrote a letter to her mother: "It was a tremendous success. Hours before I got there, every seat in the house was taken, and I was given a standing ovation throughout my speech. ☆

"If you had one dollar and you asked your father for another, how many would you have?" the teacher asked the little boy.

"One dollar," replied the boy.

"You don't know your arithmetic," said the teacher.

"No," replied the boy. "You don't know my father." ☆

How do you fire a math teacher?

Tell her she's history.

A child comes home from her first day at school. Her father asks, "Well, what did you learn today?"

The daughter replies, "Not enough. They want me to come back tomorrow." ☆

Did you hear about the delivery van loaded with thesauruses that crashed into a taxi?

Witnesses were astounded, shocked, taken aback, surprised, startled, dumbfounded, thunderstruck, caught unawares . . .

I've suffered injury, damage, harm, pain, hurt, distress...

THESAURUS

71

Sheila was called into her teacher's office for a talk.

"I'm sorry," said the teacher, "but I found out you cheated on your test, so I'm changing your A to an F. Do you have anything to say?"

"Yes," said Sheila. "That's pretty degrading." ☆

Why did the teacher put rubber bands on her students' heads?

So they could make snap decisions.

Why did the 25-watt bulb flunk out of school?

He wasn't very bright.

What did the weather announcer say about his meteorology test?

"It was a breeze with only a few foggy patches."

72

TEST
Benjamin Franklin discovered
E_____Y.

TEACHER: Class, someone has stolen my purse out of my desk. It had $100 in it. I know you're all basically good kids, so I'm willing to offer a reward of $10 to whoever returns it.

VOICE AT THE BACK OF THE ROOM: I'm offering $20!

Why are some school classes not very interesting?

Because they were developed by the BORED of Education.

Why do spiders do so well in computer class?

They love the Web.

The teacher came outside and found one of her students sitting on the ground with his hands in a giant mud puddle. "What are you doing?" asked the teacher.

The little boy looked up and said, "They say it rained an inch and three quarters last night, and I sure could use the seventy-five cents!" ☆

What kind of school does Sherlock Holmes attend?

Elementary, my dear Watson.

A kindergarten teacher watched her classroom of children while they were drawing. She occasionally walked around to see each child's work.

As she got to one little girl who was working very hard, she asked her what the drawing was.

The girl replied, "I'm drawing heaven."

The teacher paused and said, "But no one knows what heaven looks like."

Without looking up from her drawing, the girl replied, "They will in a minute." ☆

On the first day of school, the kindergarten teacher said to her class, "If anyone has to go to the bathroom, please hold up two fingers."

A little voice from the back row asked, "How will that help?" ☆

TEACHER: If you reach into your left pocket and pull out 25 cents and reach into your right pocket and pull out 40 cents, what would you have?
BILLY: Someone else's pants!

Why do ghosts make great cheerleaders?

They have lots of spirit.

73

The class was studying for a history test when one student said, "I wish we lived way back in time."

"Why is that?" asked the teacher.

"Then there would be less history to learn!" ☆

Jordan was playing in the schoolyard when he fell down and broke his right arm. Aaliyah came running up to him with a big smile on her face. "Wow, Jordan, you're so lucky. Now you don't have to take any exams."

"Actually, I'm really unlucky," replied Jordan.

"What makes you say that?" she asked.

"I'm left-handed," Jordan moaned. "I meant to fall on my other arm." ☆

74

Knock, knock.
Who's there?
Locker.
Locker who?
Locker out, but let me in!

Knock, knock.
Who's there?
Dewey.
Dewey who?
Dewey have to go to school today?

Why did the student take her math homework to gym class?
She wanted to work out her problems.

What do elves do after school?
Gnomework.

CARSON: The dog ate my homework.
TEACHER: Carson, you don't have a dog.
CARSON: It was a stray.

PEW!

The Math was OK, but the Social Studies gave me gas...

Where do you find Canada?

On a map.

TEACHER: Bobby, what happened in the year 1492?

BOBBY: I don't know. I wasn't alive back then.

TEACHER: That's enough of that, Bobby. Now, I'll give you a hint. Do *Niña, Pinta,* and *Santa Maria* sound familiar?

BOBBY: Not to me. I don't know a lot about salsa music.

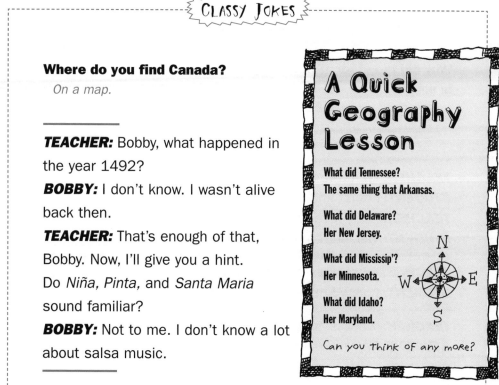

A Quick Geography Lesson

What did Tennessee?
The same thing that Arkansas.

What did Delaware?
Her New Jersey.

What did Mississip'?
Her Minnesota.

What did Idaho?
Her Maryland.

Can you think of any more?

75

Why did the student think his teacher was color-blind?

Because every time she caught him cheating, she said she was seeing red.

GEOGRAPHY TEACHER: What state would you find Lincoln in?

STUDENT: A state of extreme boredom, if he was in this class.

During which school period do cars get put together?

Assembly.

Why did the student put on eyeliner and mascara in school?

Because the teacher said she was giving the class a makeup exam.

TEACHER: What are you reading?
STUDENT: I don't know.
TEACHER: But you're reading out loud.
STUDENT: Yes, but I'm not listening!

TEACHER: What does minimum mean?
STUDENT: A very small mother.

ha-ha!

TEACHER: What is "out of bounds"?
STUDENT: An exhausted kangaroo!

Do history teachers ever marry?

No, they just get dated.

What's a history teacher's favorite quiz show?

The Dating Game.

...and Bachelor #3 is 435 Years old...

BAD APPLES
And PCs, Too!

Why did the computer cross the road?

To get a byte to eat.

What does a computer programmer eat for lunch?

An Apple!

They say that Isaac Newton discovered the law of gravity when an apple fell on his head.

Was it a laptop or a desktop model?

CUSTOMER: I cleaned my computer and now it's broken!

REPAIR TECHNICIAN: What did you clean it with?

CUSTOMER: Water and soap.

REPAIR TECHNICIAN: You're not supposed to bring water near a computer!

CUSTOMER: I don't think it was the water that broke it. . . . I think it was the spin cycle!

OK—You win! The Apple has a _much_ better operating system than Windows!

Thanks for eating at Mel's Microchips-do you want extra Silicon with that?

No, thanks - it's incompatible with my microprocessors.

Where do cool mice live?
Mousepads.

What do they serve at the cyber café?
Silicon chips with dip.

Why was Susan's dad kicking the computer?
Because he was trying to boot it up.

Where did the computer go to dance?
The Disc-o.

78

What computer sings the best?
Adele.

Why didn't the mouse cross the road?
The cord wasn't long enough.

A woman was having lunch with two friends and asked them where she could buy windows.

The first friend, who loved building things, said, "Try a hardware store."

The second friend said, "What are you talking about? Try a software store!" ☆

Steve Carell

Life magazine once celebrated Steve Carell as the funniest man alive. He got his comedic start at Denison University as a member of the student-run improvisational comedy troupe Burpee's Seedy Theatrical Company. After graduating, he joined the Chicago improv troupe the Second City and later became a cast member on *The Dana Carvey Show*. Along with fellow cast member Stephen Colbert, Carell was the voice of Gary, one half of "the Ambiguously Gay Duo." The sketch was later picked up by *Saturday Night Live (SNL)* and is credited with forging Carell's career. Carell also appeared on *The Daily Show* from 1999 to 2005, with a number of regular segments including "Even Stephen" with Stephen Colbert.

His breakout movie role came in 2004, when he played Brick Tamland, a member of Ron Burgundy's news crew, in *Anchorman: The Legend of Ron Burgundy*. In 2005, Carell signed a deal with NBC to

star in *The Office,* a mockumentary of office life. His role as Dunder Mifflin boss Michael Scott would become his most recognizable role and won him a Golden Globe Award for Best Actor in a Television Comedy Series in 2006. His uncanny ability to make even the most awkward situations funny propelled the show's popularity. His character left the show in 2011.

Not only did Carell star in a hit TV show for seven years, but he also found time to film several box office hits during that same time. His starring roles included *The 40-Year-Old Virgin* (2005), *Little Miss Sunshine* (2006), *Get Smart* (2008), and *Crazy, Stupid Love* (2011). He has also lent his voice to several animated movies, including *Over the Hedge* (2006), *Horton Hears a Who!* (2008), *Despicable Me* (2010), and *Despicable Me 2* (2013). Steve Carell is a comedian in the classic sense of the word—quite simply, he knows how to make people laugh.

How do you keep a fool busy all day?

Put him in a round room and tell him to sit in the corner!

A recent computer science graduate starts his new job at a giant computer company. He's shocked when the manager tells him that his first job will be to sweep the floor. He protests, "But I can't do that, I'm a graduate of the Super-Duper-High-Tech Institute of Technology!" The manager pauses and thinks for a second. "Well," she says, "then your first task will be to learn how to use a broom!" ☆

Why did the mother always put on a helmet before she used the computer?

Because she was afraid it would crash!

ha-ha!

How do you know when your computer has the Disney virus?

Everything in the computer goes Goofy.

A computer rolled into a bakery and went up to the counter. There were doughnuts and muffins and pastries, but the computer pointed at a plate of cookies. "Hello," it said in an electronic voice.

Astonished, the counter person replied, "Wow, we don't get too many computers in this store. Do you want some of these cookies?"

"Well," said the computer, "I might. Could you tell me how many bites are in each one?"

"I'm sorry," said the counter person. "There aren't any bytes in these cookies, just chips." ☆

Why was the computer so tired when it got home from the office?

Because it had a hard drive.

What's the fastest way to crash a computer?

Let an adult use it.

A frustrated customer calls tech support with a very tricky problem. She cannot print blue. All the other colors print fine, except blue, which is very unusual.

The tech support person on the other end tries everything he can think of to help the customer. He asks her to reinstall the program, to reboot the computer, to turn the printer on and off. None of it helps.

Finally, after hours of troubleshooting, he asks the customer if he can come by and try to resolve the problem in person. When he finally gets to her house and she shows him her computer and the printer, he instantly understands what the problem is and tells her, "From now on, print on white paper instead of blue!" ☆

81

Why were there jumper cables hooked up to Betty's computer?

She asked her dad to restart it.

What do you get when you cross Dracula with Microsoft Word?

A word count.

Alvight—who vas the viseguy who put the "Sunrise" screensaver on?

THE MAKING OF A COMEDIAN

Step 3: Uniquely You

Jokes are often based on the most humdrum items and everyday occurrences. Who would have thought a banana was funny until someone invented the slippery peel stunt or stuck one in his ear for the first time? Old-time comedian Charlie Chaplin could make anything hilarious—even a department store escalator. He had a genius for making the average person in the average situation look hysterically funny. As he said, "There is no mystery connected with 'making people laugh.' All I have ever done is to keep my eyes open and brain alert for any facts or incidents that I could use."

So look around you and think about the silly possibilities in life.

How can you tell a good computer programmer from a bad computer programmer?

The good one always comes through when the chips are down.

What did the computer keyboard say to the typist?

"You're really pushing my buttons!"

Why did the man take his computer to a clinic?

It had a virus.

Why was the disk drive so rich?

It was good at saving.

How was the computer convention?

Crowded. You couldn't get a nerd in edgewise.

Jimmy was explaining to his dad the kind of computer he wanted. "First we'll discuss hardware, and then we'll talk about the software I need."

"Wait a minute," said Jimmy's dad. "How is hardware different from software?"

Jimmy just shook his head and said, "Hardware is the part of a computer that you can kick." ✩

83

Did you hear about the computer with the corrupt hard drive?

Its backup was worse than its byte.

What do computers eat when they get hungry?

Chips.

How?

They take mega-bytes!

Why didn't the computer go to the prom?

She didn't have a data.

What do you call a computer that only types in uppercase?

SHIFTY.

84

Why did the IBM and the Apple computers get a divorce?

They weren't compatible.

How are computers like spies?

They both work in code.

Who does a baby computer cry for when she's upset?

Her motherboard.

Where are delinquent disk drives sent?

To boot camp.

How did the computer feel after its memory had been upgraded?

Chipper.

How did the computers buy a new car?
They all chipped in.

What do you get when you cross a bunny rabbit with the World Wide Web?
A hare net.

How do you compare the speeds of two computers?
Push them off the top of a building at the same time
and see which one hits the ground first.

Why did the computer get glasses?
To improve its websight.

Why did the woman attach her computer to a fishing rod?
Someone told her to hook it up.

How do you keep a nerd in suspense?
I'll tell you later!

A repair technician got a call from a computer user. The user told her that his computer was not working. He described the problems he was having, and the technician told him that his computer needed to be serviced. She told him, "Unplug the power cord and bring it here to get fixed." Later on, the man showed up at the repair shop with the power cord in his hand. ☆

How are computers like school hallways?

They both have monitors.

Why did the disk drive become a professional goalie?

It kept making great saves.

Why did the microprocessor always write form letters?

It was an impersonal computer.

How do you find a spider on the Internet?

Check out his website.

Why shouldn't you take your computer into rush-hour traffic?

Because it might crash.

PRACTICAL JOKE

Try out these greetings next time you answer the phone:

"[Your name]'s Pizza! I'm the guy if you want pie!"

"Pet's Vets! There's no business like monkey business!"

"Hello, Disco Cat, the place for glitter and litter!"

"Whine Cellar! We love to complain!"

(In a whisper) "Institute for Overly Sensitive Eardrums."

How can you tell when a fairy has been using your computer?

Pixel dust.

The queen was having problems retrieving a document from her computer. She called all her ministers into the throne room and asked them what she should do. They went away and debated for hours and hours. Finally, the ministers came up with a solution and dispatched messengers to all four points of the kingdom. These gathered every citizen they could find and brought them all to the castle. The proud ministers made all the women, men, children, and babes in arms stand in a long line and presented them to the queen. "What is the meaning of this?" the irate monarch demanded. "Why," her chief minister responded, "we thought you were looking for a single file!" ☆

87

Why did the geek turn on his computer on a hot day?

He wanted to open the Windows.

Why did the computer geek take up photography?

He wanted his own dorkroom.

Why did the boy give his teacher a PC?

The store was out of Apples.

What did the mouse say to the webcam?

Cheese!

What part of the keyboard do astronauts like best?

The space bar.

88

One afternoon, while Howard was watching over the main computer lab, he noticed a young woman sitting in front of one of the workstations with her arms crossed, staring blankly at the screen.

Fifteen minutes later, he noticed that she was still in the same position, only now she was impatiently tapping her foot. Finally, he approached her and asked if she needed help.

"Well, it's about time!" she said angrily. "I pressed the F1 button for help at least 20 minutes ago!" ☆

ha-ha!

'Snot Funny

Eeew, Gross!

What's the magic word for getting rid of scabs?
Scabracadabra!

Does it work?
Scabsolutely!

What's black and white and flat?
A panda that's been run over.

What's black and white and red all over?
A newspaper.

What else is black and white and red all over?
A zebra with a sunburn.

What were the little snots afraid of when they went to bed?
The booger man.

A man heard his friend was in the hospital but didn't know what had happened to him, or even which room to visit. So he went to the hospital and politely waited at the desk. When the nurse looked up, he gave his friend's name and asked for the room number. "Room 105, 106, 107, and 108," she replied, and went back to her paperwork.

"I don't understand," the man stammered. "Which one is it?"

"All of them," the nurse said. "He got run over by a steamroller." ☆

What's black and white and green and black and white?

Two zebras fighting over a pickle.

What's red and green and goes 80 miles an hour?

A frog in a blender.

One day a lady walked into the doctor's office. She said, "Doctor, I have a farting problem. I fart all the time. They don't smell, and they're silent. They don't even bother me! In fact, I have farted 20 times since I entered the room, and you didn't even know! Do you have a diagnosis?"

The doctor gave the lady some pills and sent her on her way. The lady came back to the doctor's office a week later and said, "Doctor! What pills did you give me? Now, when I fart, they stink!"

The doctor replied, "Great, now that we've got your sinuses cleared up, let's work on your hearing." ☆

Say "AHH..."

AHH-GH!

PRACTICAL JOKE

Scare your babysitter:

Find a big Band-Aid. Put ketchup on it and put it on yourself. Then tell the babysitter you cut yourself with a knife and were bleeding a lot, but you put a bandage on and are OK now. Then pretend to pass out.

A farmer went out to the barn to milk his cow early in the morning. He was milking away quietly and had the bucket almost half full when a bug flew into the barn and started circling his head. Suddenly, the bug flew into the cow's ear. The farmer didn't think much about it until the bug squirted out into his bucket. Looks like it went in one ear and out the udder. ☆

What do you get when you grill a Barbie doll?

A Barbieque.

91

A very pretty lady is sitting in an expensive restaurant one evening. She is waiting for her date, and wants to be sure everything is perfect. She decides to check how her hair looks. As she bends over in her chair to get a mirror from her purse, she accidentally farts quite loudly just when the waiter is walking up. She sits up, horribly embarrassed and red in the face, sure that everyone in the restaurant has heard the fart. She tries to blame it on the waiter, and turns to him and orders, "Stop that!" The waiter looks at her calmly and replies, "Sure, lady. Where was it headed?" ☆

Darn! There go my party outfit and all my accessories!

What's green and blue and yellow and black?

A burnt peacock.

A teacher tells her second-grade class that she is going to teach them a new word today. She tells them that the word is *definitely* and its meaning is "that something is without a doubt."

She then asks the class if anyone can think of a sentence with *definitely* in it. She sees little Kelly, who is in the back raising her hand, quite sure of herself, and asks for her sentence.

Kelly stands up and says, "The sky is definitely blue."

The teacher replies to her, "Well, that's a good sentence, but sometimes the sky is cloudy or gray, so the sky is not definitely blue. Anyone else?"

David's hand flies up and she calls on him. David answers, "Water is definitely clear."

"Well, David, while that's a good sentence, sometimes water is muddy or cloudy, so it's not definitely clear. Anyone else?"

Finally, looking very unsure, little Billy slowly raises his hand.

"Yes, Billy?" asks the teacher.

"Can I ask a question, teacher?" Billy replies.

"Yes, of course."

"Do farts have lumps?"

"No. Why do you ask?"

"Because if they don't, then I've definitely pooped in my pants." ☆

What is brown and sticky?

A stick.

Ben Stiller

Ben Stiller has comedy in his blood—he is the son of two famous comedians, husband-and-wife comedy team Jerry Stiller and Anne Meara. Stiller grew up in Hollywood, shooting home movies with a Super 8 camera when not producing plays with his sister, Amy. Ben began his showbiz career as a comedian, and he has also made a name for himself in Hollywood as an actor, writer, producer, and director. He started climbing the ladder when, as a young man, he wrote and produced his own sketch-comedy television show, *The Ben Stiller Show*, for MTV, which launched his career and won him several awards. He later directed and starred in the film *Reality Bites* (1994).

Since then, Stiller has played a handsome but dumb supermodel in *Zoolander* (2001) and *Zoolander 2* (2016), and a museum security guard who discovers that the exhibits come to life when no one else is around in *Night at the Museum* (2006) and it's sequels. He also gives voice to Alex the lion in the *Madagascar* series of animated films, which tell the story of a crew of zoo animals who learn how to survive in the wild.

Stiller's comic genius lies in his ability to create very realistic characters who find themselves in very funny situations. Despite his success in comedy, Stiller says, "I've never really felt like a funny, funny guy. I've never been Mr. Life of the Party." Clearly, juggling five professions makes you very humble!

BEHIND THE PUNCH LINE:

Impersonations

Have you ever heard someone with a funny voice on TV or in a movie, and then tried to mimic his or her voice? That's an *impersonation*. A comedian who is really talented at impersonations can often imitate not only someone's voice, but their gestures, their mannerisms, and even their clothing style down to the last detail.

Comedians who do impersonations aren't trying to fool their audiences into believing that they actually are someone else, as an actor in a film might. It's more important to exaggerate things that make the other person so recognizable—a squeaky voice, hair twirling, or a prop like a cane or a doll—than to nail the person's character exactly. It also helps to pick someone who is very famous, so the audience will be sure to get the joke. If the audience is just family, try to get a bigger laugh by imitating your big sister on the phone with her boyfriend or your mom talking to a client.

Many famous comedians have made careers out of their ability to impersonate others. Most skits on *Saturday Night Live* and other sketch comedy shows feature players who create characters based on real people. Try it—you'll like it!

94

Chuck goes in to his doctor and says, "Doctor, I'm a little embarrassed to talk about this, but I seem to be barfing a lot."

The doctor says, "Well, I'm glad you feel you can bring this up, Chuck." ☆

Why was the car smelly?

It had too much gas.

What animal is always getting food poisoning?

The yak.

Why did Tigger stick his head in the toilet?

He was looking for Pooh.

What do you get when you cross a mouth with a tornado?

A tongue twister.

It was a beautiful summer in Switzerland, and all the Swiss cows were enjoying excellent grass crops. There was more than enough grass to go around, and all through the rivers and dells, you could hear the cows mooing with happiness. But sometime in late July, there arrived a band of roughhousing moose who muscled the cows out of the way and began eating more grass than was seemingly possible. Then, just when it looked like things couldn't get worse, the moose started to throw up all over the place, nauseated from their grassy feasting. For the rest of the summer, the farmers could be heard complaining that "the hills are alive with the sounds of moose sick!" ☆

15

I zink I'm going to be sick!

Silly Song

(Sung to the tune of "When the Saints Go Marching In")

Oh when the ants
Get in our food,
It puts us in an awful mood.
We find legs in our egg salad,
When the ants get in our food.

Oh when the dog
Drools on our meal,
To eat at all loses all appeal.
We find slobber on our sandwich,
When the dog drools on our meal.

Oh when the sand
Gets in our lunch,
Potato chips have extra crunch.
We find grit in ground-beef patties,
When the sand gets in our lunch.

Oh when the flies
Land on our spread,
We've no desire to be fed.
We find bugs on our bologna,
When the flies land on our spread.

Next time we dine
We'll stay inside.
Our hungry mouths we'll open wide.
Within walls, it's safe to swallow,
Next time we'll dine inside.

97

Another Silly Song

Everybody's doin' it, doin' it, doin' it;
Pickin' their noses and a-chewin' it.
You think it's some kinda candy
But it's snot.

What do you call a boy who's been half eaten by a Python?

The Name Game

What do you call a girl with one leg? *Eileen.*

What do you call a boy with no arms and no legs on the front porch? *Matt.*

What do you call a man in a tiger's cage? *Claude.*

What do you call a boy hanging on the wall? *Art.*

What do you call a boy floating in the pool? *Bob.*

What do you call a girl with a wooden leg? *Peg.*

What do you call a boy who's been caught by a tribe of cannibals? *Stu.*

18

Les.

ROCKET SCIENCE

All the Mysteries of Outer Space, Made More Confusing

Darth Vader and Luke Skywalker were duking it out somewhere in space. Darth Vader said to Luke, "Join me and experience the power of the dark side!"

Luke replied, "The dark side can't be that powerful."

"Yes it is. I even know what you're getting for Christmas, Luke."

"How?" Luke asked.

"I felt your presents." ☆

BZZZZT!..

WHOA! Thanks for the lightsaber, Darth-Dude! It even cuts through fruitcake!

Why did the earthling fall in love with the alien?

Because she was out of this world!

Why did Captain Kirk sneak into the ladies' room?

He wanted to go where no man had gone before.

Why did the atom cross the road?

Because it was time to split.

BEHIND THE PUNCH LINE:
The Funny Pages

When you read the comic strips every Sunday, do you think about the artists as comedians? Probably not—but they are. They use paper and pen rather than their voices and bodies to make people laugh.

Charles Schulz, who wrote *Peanuts* for fifty consecutive years until his death in 2000, managed to give each one of his characters a distinctly funny and different personality. There was Charlie Brown, the eternally optimistic loser; Lucy, the grumpy meanie; Linus, who liked to be left alone; and Sally, the romantic, among others. Garry Trudeau, the author of *Doonesbury*, uses his pen to poke fun at politics. *Dilbert* cartoonist Scott Anderson makes light of office jobs. And the list goes on.

What are your favorite comic strips? Next time you look at one, think about the artist applying the steps in this book in order to express a perfectly timed joke. You will see that comedy comes through in writing as well as it does in spoken words.

Why couldn't the astronauts book a room on the moon?

Because it was full.

What did the alien say to the pop bottle?

"Take me to your liter."

What did the alien say to the tree?

"Take me to your cedar."

What did the sun say when it was introduced to the earth?

"Pleased to heat you."

A robot mother and daughter walk by a hardware store, and the daughter stops to admire the paint cans displayed in the window. "I'm sorry," says the mother robot, "but your old coat will have to last you another year." ☆

What do you call a robot that always takes the longest route?

R2 Detour.

How did the scientist invent bug spray?

She started from scratch.

Sherlock Holmes and his trusty associate Watson were on a camping trip. They had gone to bed and were lying there looking up at the sky. Holmes said, "Watson, look up and tell me what you see."

"Well, I see thousands of stars," he replied.

"And what does that tell you?" asked Holmes.

"I guess it means we're going to have another nice day tomorrow. What does it mean to you?"

"To me, it means that someone has stolen our tent." ☆

What did the alien say to the tabby cat?
"Take me to your litter."

What did the alien say to the eggs?

"Take me to your beater."

What did the astronaut think of the takeoff?
She thought it was a blast.

How come aliens don't drown in hot chocolate?
They sit on the Mars-mallows.

One day, a flying saucer lands in Times Square and tries to park in the middle of the sidewalk. Immediately a traffic cop rushes over to the Martian and says, "You can't park that thing here. Go find a legal spot."

The Martian looks up and says, "Take me to your meter." ☆

No driver's License, No License plate, No vehicle registration...

102

Chris Rock

Chris Rock has gained fame as a sassy, wacky, pop-culture expert. His witty commentary on current events has made him a comedy star for the MTV generation.

A teenage Rock was initiated into the Manhattan comedy club scene as a protégé of much-admired comic Eddie Murphy. Rock followed Murphy's career path to *Saturday Night Live,* where Rock appeared from 1990 to 1993.

Rock's comedy style has stayed true to Murphy's early style as well. He's raw and rebellious, but with a sophisticated edge that comes from closely watching the nightly news. He frequently tackles tough issues like race and poverty in his comedy routines and isn't afraid to make people angry to make a point.

After *SNL,* Rock produced several comedy specials that ran on the cable channel HBO. He has also appeared in several films, including *Down to Earth* (2001), *The Longest Yard* (2005), *Grown Ups* (2010), and *What to Expect When You're Expecting* (2012). Rock's frequent appearances on HBO and several award shows have created a solid fan base and cemented his status in the comedy world. He's also gained a following thanks to his cartoon voice-overs, such as the cold and flu fighter Osmosis in *Osmosis Jones* (2001) and Marty the zebra in the animated features *Madagascar* (2005), *Madagascar 2* (2008), and *Madagascar 3: Europe's Most Wanted* (2012). From sophisticated political comedy to cartoon antics, Chris Rock knows how to make people laugh.

What's bright yellow, has a long tail, and flies through the sky?

EARTHLING: We put a man on the moon in 1969.
MARTIAN: Big deal! We're going to put a team on the sun.
EARTHLING: You're crazy! They'll burn up before they even get close.
MARTIAN: We're not that stupid! We're sending them up at night!

How do you get an astronaut's baby to stop crying?

Comet.

Why did the Martian leave the Mars party?

He didn't like the atmosphere.

How do you know when your little brother's an alien?

He can change TV channels from the sofa without using the remote.

How do you know when your older sister's an alien?

She always knocks before coming into your room.

HALLEY'S CANARY.

WATCH YOUR STEP

How do you throw the best bash in the universe?

Planet.

How do you throw the best concert in the universe?

Rocket.

How did the astronaut feel when he ran into the alien with six lasers for arms?

Stunned.

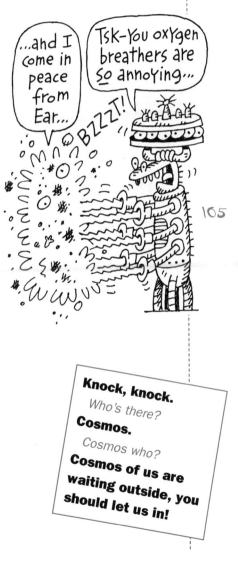

...and I come in peace from Ear...

Tsk—You oxygen breathers are *so* annoying...

BZZZT!

105

How does the man on the moon trim his hedge?

Eclipse it.

What sporting event do people from Venus, Mars, Saturn, and Mercury watch on TV every October?

The Out-of-This-World Series.

Why is football so popular on Venus?

Because all the houses have Astroturf on their front lawns.

What's the best hockey team in the universe?

The All-Stars.

Knock, knock.
Who's there?
Cosmos.
Cosmos who?
Cosmos of us are waiting outside, you should let us in!

What's the difference between Neptune and Earth?

There's a world of difference!

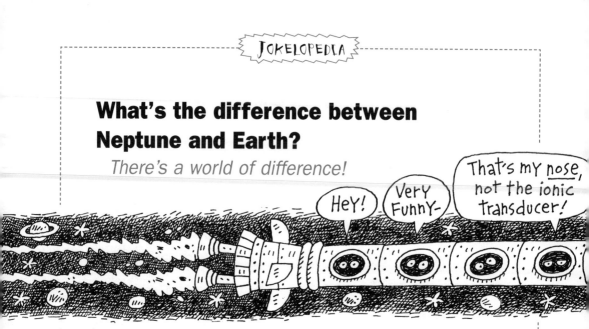

Hey!

Very Funny—

That's my <u>nose</u>, not the ionic transducer!

How do astronauts take their kids to school?

In space station wagons.

What happens to astronauts who misbehave?

They're grounded.

What does an astronaut use to dust those hard-to-reach black holes?

A vacuum cleaner.

What did Neptune say to Saturn?

Give me a ring sometime.

Helpful Hint

I f anyone ever makes fun of you for wearing glasses, tell them you have a very high-tech titanium alloy detachable face and that you need the hooks in your glasses to keep your face attached to the rest of your head.

Why was the spacecraft reading the horoscopes?

It was a Gemini.

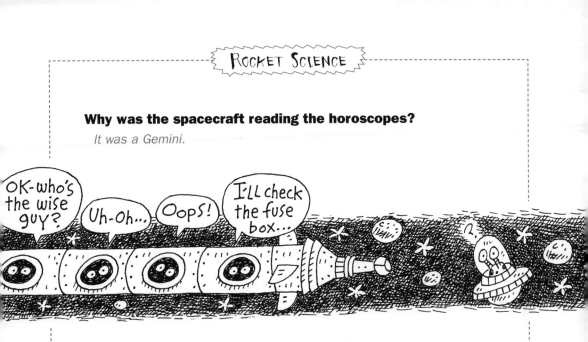

orbert Lagenfeld was a mad scientist who was thought to be creating replicas of himself in his laboratory. This was making some of the townsfolk anxious, so they gathered whatever they could and proceeded up the hill to confront him. The town stationer was armed with a box of pens, the librarian with a pile of books, and a handful of farmers had heavy sacks of wheat slung over their shoulders.

When they got to Lagenfeld's mansion, they encountered dozens of replicas of the mad scientist running amok. The townsfolk set upon them, killing Lagenfeld's creations left and right. The stationer poked them with her pens, the librarian clobbered them over the head with his books. Meanwhile, the farmers were hitting the replicas with the sacks of wheat. Soon the townsfolk collapsed in exhaustion, their work done—but off in the distance they saw Lagenfeld himself jump into his car. The few farmers with any energy left heaved their bags toward the car, but the bags broke open harmlessly and Lagenfeld made his getaway. As he vanished into the distance, they could hear him cry: "Bics and tomes may break my clones, but grains will never harm me." ✪

107

How do you turn a regular scientist into a mad scientist?

Step on her toes.

How do you know when you're talking to a mad scientist and her clone?

They they say say everything everything twice twice.

What do you carve on a robot's tombstone?

Rust in peace.

How do spacemen hold up their pants?

With asteroid belts.

Why did the silly astronaut turn off all the lights on the spaceship?

He wanted to travel at the speed of dark.

What do you get when you cross a potato with a rocket ship?

Spudnik.

Knock, knock.
Who's there?
Apollo.
Apollo who?
Apollo-gize for not answering sooner!

FAMILY FUNNIES

Brothers, Sisters, and Aunts of Step-uncles

DAD: When Abraham Lincoln was your age, he walked miles to school, uphill, in the snow, every day.
SON: Yeah? Well, when Abraham Lincoln was your age, Dad, he was president!

DAD 1: My son is so smart, I think he's more intelligent than the president.
DAD 2: Why do you say that?
DAD 1: Well, he could recite the Gettysburg Address when he was ten. Lincoln didn't recite it until he was fifty.

DAD: Today we celebrate Abraham Lincoln's birthday. Some people called him Honest Abe.
DAUGHTER: If he was so honest, then why do they close all the banks and keep kids home from school?

Four-score and seven years ago, or the polynomial inverse of the equivalent numerator, our forefathers...

What's the difference between a dog who sticks his head out the car window and your little brother or sister?

One's a neck in the pane, the other's a pain in the neck.

What did the pantyhose say to the nylons at the family reunion?

"Wow, we really run in the family."

110

A little boy returned from the grocery store with his mom. While his mom put away the groceries, the little boy opened his box of animal crackers and spread them all over the kitchen table.

"What are you doing?" asked his mom.

"The box says you shouldn't eat them if the seal is broken," said the little boy. "I'm looking for the seal." ✩

*A*n elderly couple died in their sleep after long lives and found themselves in heaven. After greeting them, Saint Peter took them on a tour of their new environment. He said, "Here is your seaside condo; and over there are the swimming pools, tennis courts, and two golf courses. If you need any drinks, just stop by any of the many bars located all around the area."

After Saint Peter was done and had walked off, the old man turned to his wife and said angrily, "Heck, Millie, we could have been here 15 years ago if you hadn't made us eat all that stupid oat bran, wheat germ, and low-fat food!" ✩

The daughter of a famous basketball star was watching television and her dad was in the other room. "Dad, come here! Mom's on the television again!" yelled the little girl.

Her dad yelled back, "You just tell Mom to get off the television and sit on the couch like a normal adult." ☆

A mom walks into a store and asks if she could have a toy tractor for her daughter. The store clerk replies, "I'm sorry, ma'am, but we don't do exchanges." ☆

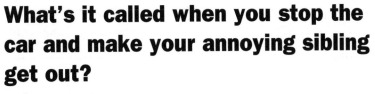

OUCH! ACK! OOF!

What's it called when you stop the car and make your annoying sibling get out?

A pest stop.

A little girl became ill and was taken to the hospital. It was her first time away from home and she began to cry. The nurse was concerned and asked the little girl if she was homesick.

"No," said the girl. "I'm here sick!" ☆

M ary's husband lost his job as a tailor in a local shop, but he didn't talk much about it. He didn't seem to be too bothered, though, and Mary was so curious that she finally asked, "Why is it that you're not working as a tailor anymore, Bill?"

Bill thought a moment and then he said, "Well, I guess it didn't really suit me. It was a sew-sew job." ☆

112

"I am going to be a famous magician," said Eddie to his father, "because I can make a golf ball float."

Eddie's father was very curious. "And how do you do that?" he asked.

"Well, it's very scientific. It requires some magic ingredients," said Eddie.

Eddie's father leaned forward in his chair. "Oh, really," he said. "And what are they?"

"Well, the golf ball, of course. And then two scoops of ice cream and some root beer." ☆

Hmm—that vanilla's pretty thick—better get my nine iron...

BEHIND THE PUNCH LINE:
Vaudeville

Vaudeville is a French word meaning a popular, comic song. The term eventually came to mean a comedy show featuring a collection of variety acts—singers as well as dancers, acrobats, comedians, mimes, ventriloquists, and performing animals. Skits and short plays were also part of the elaborate shows.

Vaudeville was one of the most popular forms of entertainment during the early part of the twentieth century. In 1919, there were more than 900 theaters in the country featuring vaudeville shows. At that time, movies were still new and they had no sound, since no one had figured out how to combine sounds with the pictures yet. Most working actors of that time performed in vaudeville shows. However, as new technology came along, "talkies"—movies with sound—appeared and became very popular. They became so popular that vaudeville shows were kicked out of their theaters to make room for movie screens.

It is a shame that live theater like vaudeville became less popular as the movie industry grew larger. Vaudeville shows allowed actors to interact with the audience and to see firsthand what made the fans laugh. If a part of the show wasn't funny, it could be replaced with something else, so no two shows were exactly the same.

A dad goes into a pet store and asks if he can return the puppy he got for his son. The owner replies, "I'm sorry, sir, but we've already sold your son to someone else." ✩

_L_ittle Sally always looked forward to her lunch, and today Sally's mom was excited about the new treat she had planned for Sally. Sally's mom laid a carefully arranged plate on the table and then went to the kitchen to get some napkins. She was completely confused when she came back to see Sally crying at the table.

"What's wrong, Sally? Don't you like the animal crackers I bought for you?" asked her mom.

Sally just cried even harder and wailed, "But Mommy, we're vegetarians!" ☆

What did the tomato dad say to his tomato son who was lagging behind?
   "Ketchup!"

How did the giant's wife know that Jack was coming?

She could hear Jack and the beans talk!

_A_ teenager tells his father, "There's trouble with the car. It has water in the carburetor."

The father looks confused and says, "Water in the carburetor? That's ridiculous."

But the son insists. "I tell you the car has water in the carburetor."

His father is starting to get a little nervous. "You don't even know what a carburetor is," he says. "I'll check it out. Where's the car?"

"In the pool." ☆

A father and his small daughter were standing in front of the tiger's cage at the zoo. The dad was explaining how ferocious and strong tigers are, and the little girl was listening to him with a very serious expression.

"Daddy," she said finally, "if the tiger got out of his cage and ate you up. . ."

"Yes, dear?" asked the father.

"Which bus would I take home?" ☆

Where do snowmen and snowwomen go to dance?

The snowball.

T wo mothers were comparing stories about their children. The first one complained that her son never wanted to get out of bed in the morning. The second told her, "I don't have that problem. When it's time for my son to get up, I just throw the cat in his bed."

"How does that help?" asked the first mom.

"He sleeps with the dog." ☆

115

A little boy was practicing the violin in the living room while his mother was trying to read in the den. The family dog was lying in the den, and as the screeching sounds of the violin reached the dog's ears, he began to howl loudly. The mother listened to the dog and the violin for as long as she could. Then she jumped up, dropped her paper to the floor, and shouted above the noise, "For goodness' sake, can't you play something the dog doesn't know?" ☆

...and to interpret Mozart correctly, one must play from the heart!

A man bought his wife a talking bird for her birthday. It spoke seven languages and cost him a month's pay. "Well," he asked her when he got home, "did you get the bird I sent you?"

"Yes," answered his wife. "I already have it in the oven."

"What! That bird could speak seven languages!" said the man, upset.

"Then why didn't it say anything?" ☆

The Marx Brothers

The Marx Brothers were a comedy team of brothers—Groucho, Chico, Harpo, Gummo, and Zeppo—who first gained notice for their use of improvisation onstage. The brothers were organized into an act in 1914 by their mother, who often performed with them in vaudeville shows. The brothers (except for Gummo, who quit the act in 1924 and was replaced by younger brother Zeppo) appeared on Broadway in 1924 in a show called *I'll Say She Is.* During the show, the Marx Brothers made up most of their lines on the spot and even talked to the audience from the stage; they rarely used the script. People attended the show over and over because no two performances were ever alike.

The brothers' first film, *The Cocoanuts,* was created from another Broadway show. It opened in 1929, and the Marx Brothers immediately became movie stars. During the 1930s, they made a movie a year. Movies like *Animal Crackers, Duck Soup,* and *A Night at the Opera* showcased the Marxes' flawless comic timing. Although the brothers were not able to improvise as much in films as they did onstage, their easy interaction with one another on the movie screen made it seem as if they were.

What do you get when you cross your brother with an owl?

A wise guy.

A little girl came home early from school, so her father asked her why.

"Because I was the only one who could answer a question," she told him.

"What question was that?" said her father.

"Who threw the paper airplane at the teacher?" ☆

118

Why did Billy's brother run to the refrigerator when Billy asked him to play?

Because his favorite game was freeze tag.

One day a little girl put her shoes on by herself for the first time. Her mother noticed that her left shoe was on her right foot.

"Honey," said the mom, "I think your shoes are on the wrong feet."

The little girl looked up and said, "No, Mom, I *know* these are my feet." ☆

A suspicious husband hires a private detective to check up on his wife. The husband tells the detective that he wants not only a written account but also as many videos of her in any kind of compromising situations as the detective can get.

Two weeks later the detective calls the man and tells him to meet at his office, that he has all the evidence he needs. The man hurries to the detective's office and they sit together watching the videos. The first video shows the man's wife meeting another man, and the two of them are walking in the park, laughing. Another video shows her with a different man, smiling and dancing.

All together, he watches videos of his wife involved in dozens of different activities, each with a different man, each time appearing extremely happy. "Amazing," said the husband, in shock. "Simply amazing! I just can't believe it."

"I'm so sorry," the detective said. "It makes us think we can never really know anyone, even those so close to us."

"I know!" replied the man, still in shock. "I really never knew my wife could be so much fun." ✩

A boy was riding in the elevator of a very tall building with his parents. He tugged on his father's coat and, when his father bent over, asked him a question.

The father frowned and shook his head. The little boy tugged on his father's coat again and asked the same question.

"No," said the father.

When the little boy tugged on his father's coat a third time, the father lost his patience and said, "I don't care how Superman does it! We're going up this way!" ✩

Why do parents carry their babies?

Because babies aren't big enough to carry their parents.

Little Doris went to visit the new baby at the Johnsons' house. Mrs. Johnson answered the door and Doris said, "Hi, Mrs. Johnson, is baby Bobby there? Could I talk to him?"

Mrs. Johnson smiled and said, "I'm sorry but Bobby is only a little baby. He can't talk yet."

Doris said, "That's OK. I'll wait." ☆

What did the paint give the wall on their first anniversary?
A new coat.

Why did the pregnant woman race to the hospital?

She wanted to have a speedy delivery.

When should you bring your father to class?
When you have a pop quiz.

"Are caterpillars good to eat?" asked a little boy at the dinner table.

"No," said his father. "What makes you ask a question like that?"

"You had one on your salad, but it's gone now." ✩

Why was the margarine unhappy when she gave birth to the marmalade?

She was expecting something butter.

Jack couldn't mow the lawn yesterday because he sprained his ankle. What do you think his dad said to that?

"That's a lame excuse!"

121

PRACTICAL JOKE

Tell someone that you can pin a glass of water to the wall. Naturally, your victim will not believe you, so you set out to prove it. You will need a glass (a real glass, not a paper cup) of water and a straight pin. Hold the glass up and start pinning it up—then drop the pin. Ask your victim very nicely to please pick up the pin for you. When he or she bends over to get the pin, pour the water on his or her head.

S ally's parents were going out, and Sally said, "For twenty bucks, Dad, I'll be good."

"Oh, please," said her father. "When I was your age, I was good for nothing." ✩

A man calls his brother with a request. He says, "As you know, I'm going on a business trip soon, and if my wife gives birth while I'm away, I want you to name the twins."

"It'll be an honor to do that for you," replies the brother.

A month later the brother calls with news that the twins were born. "Your wife gave birth to a beautiful girl and a handsome boy," says the brother.

"That's wonderful! What did you call them?" the man asks.

"I called the girl Deniece," says the brother.

"That's very pretty. And what did you call the boy?" asks the man.

"I called the boy De nephew." ✩

122

W hile on duty, a lifeguard noticed a small boy peeing in the pool and went to inform the boy's mother. He asked the mother to make her young son stop urinating in the pool.

"Everyone knows," the mother replied to him, "that from time to time, young children will urinate in a pool."

"Maybe so," said the lifeguard. "But not usually from the diving board!" ✩

Three old men have just arrived in heaven and are attending an orientation meeting. They are all asked, "When you are at the funeral and your friends and families are mourning, what would you like to hear them say about you?"

The first guy says, "I'd like to hear them say that I was a great doctor and a great family man."

The second guy says, "I would like them to say that I was a wonderful husband and schoolteacher, and that I made a huge difference in our children of tomorrow."

The last guy thinks a moment and says, "I think I'd like to hear them say 'Look! He's moving!'" ☆

123

A bully is picking on a boy's sister. The boy runs up and pushes the bully away, saying, "Stop picking on my sister—that's my job!" ☆

When do mothers have baby boys?

On Son-days.

Why did the little girl bury her father and mother?

She wanted to grow a family tree.

What do weathermen call their baby boys?

Sunny.

A husband and wife were driving their RV across the country and were nearing a town called Kissimmee. They noted the strange spelling and tried to figure out how to pronounce it: KISS-i-me, kiss-I-me, kiss-i-ME. They grew more and more confused as they drove into the town. Because they were hungry, they pulled into a restaurant to get something to eat. At the counter, the man said to the server: "My wife and I can't figure out how to pronounce the name of this place. Will you tell me where we are and say it very slowly so that I can understand?"

The server looked at him and said: "Buuurrrgerrrr Kiiiinnnng." ☆

124

OBJECTS OF AMUSEMENT

Household Items Unite

What did one plate say to the other?
"Dinner's on me."

What did one wall say to the other?
"Meet me at the corner."

Why couldn't the tire quit its job?

It was flat broke.

Why did the kid throw quarters under the car wheel?
He wanted to help change a tire.

Why did the stoplight turn red?
Wouldn't you if you had to change in the middle of the street?

Aaah! You're a cake and ice cream MESS, young man! You just march yourself into the dishwasher this instant!

Why was everyone worried about the small bucket?

It was a little pail.

What did one toilet say to the other?

What has one horn and gives milk?

A milk truck.

Did you hear the one about the knives?

It's a cutup.

Did you hear about the jigsaw puzzle that got fired?

It went to pieces.

How do you get a tissue to dance?

Put a little boogey in it.

What did the quilt say to the bed?

"I've got you covered."

What did the shirt say to the sock in the dryer?

"I'll see you next time around."

Why did the scientist install a knocker on her door?

She wanted to win the no-bell prize.

You look a little flushed!

WAYS TO DESCRIBE A NOT-SO-SMART PERSON

(they'll never know it's an insult!):

Not the sharpest knife in the drawer.

Not the sharpest tool in the shed.

Not the brightest bulb on the Christmas tree.

(S)he fell out of the stupid tree
and hit all the branches on the way down.

One fry shy of a Happy Meal.

A few sandwiches short of a picnic.

A few sodas short of a six-pack.

A few grapes short of a bunch.

The wheel is spinning, but the hamster's dead.

A few bricks short of a load.

A few cards short of a deck.

The elevator doesn't go all the way to the top.

There! These holes should make me Lighter!

What happened to the leopard that fell in the washer?
He came out spotless.

Why did the house go to the doctor?
Because it had a window pane.

Did you hear about the ice that lost its job?
It was crushed.

Did you hear about the underwear that lost its job?
It was bummed.

128

What do you put in a barrel to make it lighter?
A hole.

What did the rope say after it tangled?
"Oh no, knot again!"

Why couldn't the bell keep a secret?
It always tolled.

What climbs trees without a sound and has feet that always touch the ground?
A vine.

What has teeth but doesn't bite?
A comb.

Ellen DeGeneres

Before Ellen DeGeneres got her own daytime talk show, she did stand-up comedy, beginning her career at a club close to home, in New Orleans. It was just a few years later, in 1982, that a taped club performance helped launch her onto the national map, earning her the honor of Showtime's "Funniest Person in America."

By 1989, DeGeneres had moved to Los Angeles and decided to give acting a try. She landed the part of the title character in the groundbreaking sitcom *Ellen,* which ran from 1994 to 1998 and earned a number of awards and nominations. Since then she's been in a number of films (in 2003, she was the voice of Dory, the lovable fish with incredibly short-term memory in the clever animated feature *Finding Nemo*), hosted numerous awards shows, and even authored two *New York Times*–bestselling books, *My Point . . . And I Do Have One* (1995), and *The Funny Thing Is . . .* (2003),

and published a third book, *Seriously . . . I'm Kidding* (2011).

DeGeneres soon returned to what she loves best—stand-up. Never one to turn down something new, however, she may have found a new love in 2003 with the start of her very own talk show. Her loyal fans tune in daily to watch her on *The Ellen DeGeneres Show.* Her audiences love her sincerity, directness, and most of all, her wry sense of humor—most of which comes from her unique observations on the absurdity of everyday life. She does silly dances at the beginning of each program, showing that she doesn't take herself too seriously. And the funny bone just may be genetic—her brother, Vance, was a correspondent for Comedy Central's *The Daily Show* with Jon Stewart (a funny take on real news topics) for several years. Ellen DeGeneres— comedian, actor, and daytime talk-show host extraordinaire. Is there anything she can't do?

OK—hand over all your cushions, Sofa-boy! C'mon—I ain't got all day!

Why was the couch afraid of the chair?

The chair was armed.

What did the bald man say when he got a comb for his birthday?

"I'll never part with it."

What gets wetter as it dries?

A towel.

What did the 0 say to the 8?

"Nice belt."

How can you get four suits for a dollar?

Buy a deck of cards.

Why shouldn't you hang a funny picture on your wall?

The plaster might crack up.

What did the lightbulb say to the switch?

"You turn me on."

What has a head and a tail but no body?

A coin!

NEW SHOELACE: Why are you crying, Old Shoelace?
Can't you tie a bow?
OLD SHOELACE: No, I'm a frayed knot.

Why did the boy eat the lamp?

His mother told him to have a light snack.

ha-ha!

What is a soda machine's favorite dance?

The can-can!

131

What do you throw out when you need it and take in when you don't need it?

An anchor.

What driver doesn't need a license?

A screwdriver!

> Get this belt sander moving before the hardware store finds out we're gone!

OFF ON
CLICK!

One day, a housework-challenged husband decided to wash his favorite shirt. Upon entering the laundry room, he shouted to his wife, "What setting do I use on the washing machine?"

"It depends," she replied. "What does it say on your shirt?"

He yelled back, "UCLA." ☆

What did the couch say halfway through the marathon?

"Sofa, so good."

What did the carpet say to the floor?

"Don't move. I've got you covered."

132

A man is locked in a room with no way to get out. In the room are a piano, a saw, a table, and a baseball bat. How could he get out?

He could take a key from the piano and unlock the door.

He could take the bat and get three strikes. Then he'd be out.

He could take the saw and cut the table in two. Then by putting the two halves together, he would have a "hole" and he could get out. ☆

What do you call an angle that's gotten into a car crash?

A rectangle.

Why isn't red happy to see purple?

It starts to feel blue.

What kind of bow is impossible to tie?

A rainbow.

PATIENT: Doctor, I think I'm a dog.
DOCTOR: Have a seat on the couch and we'll talk about it.
PATIENT: I can't. I'm not allowed on the furniture!

Why are riddles like pencils?

They're no good unless they have a point!

What happens when you throw a clock in the air?

Time's up!

What did the big clock say to his shy son?

"Take your hands off your face."

Why did Bobby tie a clock to his palms?

He wanted to have time on his hands.

Why did the cabinet go to the psychiatrist?

It kept talking to its shelf.

...and all day LONG, it's dishes IN, dishes OUT! SLAM! SLAM! SLAM!

Yes...und you are starting to get a handle on zis problem?

PRACTICAL JOKES

Slumber-party jokes to try:

1. Wait until some unlucky person has the nerve to fall asleep first. Take a glass of warm water and carefully place his or her hand into the water. Wait.

Warning: This joke is supposed to make the victim wet the bed. Try this only if you are prepared to tackle the cleanup.

2. If a friend is sleeping in a four-poster bed, wait until he or she is asleep. Take a ball of yarn and wrap it around and around the bedposts, until your victim appears to be sleeping in a spider web. The reaction when the person wakes up and can't get out of bed: priceless.

134

3. If you have a friend who gets up to pee in the middle of the night, stretch plastic wrap tightly over the toilet bowl. Make sure there aren't any wrinkles or holes. Put the seat down over the edges of the plastic wrap. Wait.

4. Pour cold water over the shower curtain rod on someone using the shower. Run away fast.

5. Put some fake plastic vomit in the sink. When this stuff is wet, it looks amazingly real. Expect lots of screaming.

...back in a minute, I've got to use the

I Love Lucy and Lucille Ball

I *Love Lucy* is considered the first-ever sitcom. The show, which first aired in 1951, starred a red-headed comedienne named Lucille Ball as Lucy Ricardo, a housewife whose crazy antics drove her husband, Ricky, nuts. Ball was married to Cuban musician and actor Desi Arnaz, who played her husband on the show. (It must have been a difficult transition!) Ball's slapstick acting style, combined with some very funny writing, made *I Love Lucy* a landmark of American television. One episode of *I Love Lucy* featured Lucy and her friend Ethel working in a candy factory. They were supposed to fill boxes with candy as it came off a conveyor belt. When the machine broke and began spewing candy everywhere, Lucy had to stuff the candies down her dress. Wacky, yes—but what else was she supposed to do? *I Love Lucy* was one of the first television programs to focus on relationships—between husbands and wives, between neighbors, and between friends. Nearly every sitcom on TV today can trace its development back to *I Love Lucy.*

DANGER
BE CAREFUL
WHEN BELT
IS IN MOTION.

A genius was working on a new invention. It was such a great machine that it could perform twenty tasks at once. It could water a garden, pour milk, sew buttons on a coat, scrub dishes, squirt ketchup, walk the dog, solve math problems, catch flies, bake cakes, stamp envelopes and lick them shut, find lost keys, tie shoelaces, change a baby's diaper, play dodgeball, fold laundry, make hot-fudge sundaes, clean the cat's litter box, turn on the radio, plant petunias, and answer the phone. The genius had all the parts laid out in front of her, but needed something to put the machine together. So she sent her dumb assistant to the store to buy some glue. The store had almost everything—toothpaste, vacuum cleaners, cream soda, breaded halibut, licorice, but no glue. The assistant wasn't upset. She just bought the breaded halibut.

How come?

It doesn't take a genius to know fish sticks. ✩

Why was the flight late?

It forgot its staircase.

What happens to spoons who work too much?

They go stir-crazy.

Why did the watch go on vacation?

To unwind.

Marcia asked Bill, "Was that the clock tocking earlier?"

"Not to me," said Bill. "It wouldn't even give me the time of day."

THE MAKING OF A COMEDIAN

Step 4: Plotting Your Strategy

If you were able to convince someone to buy you this book, you've mastered the first principle of joke telling: strategy. Strategy is one of the most important tools in the comedian's box of tricks. It's how you plan your act to make people laugh when you want them to laugh.

The secret to influencing others is to have confidence in yourself. You are the one onstage, under the spotlight—you have the power. So don't apologize before you tell a joke—especially one that comes from this book.

What do windows do when a big gust of wind comes?

They shutter.

What accidents happen every 24 hours?

Day breaks and night falls.

Did you hear about the crimes over at that house they're renovating?

The shower was stalled while the curtains were held up. Apparently the doors were also hung, and I heard the window was framed for it. ☆

137

What made the newspaper blush?

It saw the comic strip.

Why was the dresser embarrassed?

Its drawers fell down.

Why was the nail so unhappy?

The carpenter kept hitting it on the head.

138

What nail does a carpenter hate to hit?

Her thumbnail.

What did the refrigerator say to the milk?

"Now, don't get fresh with me."

Randy and Matt set out for a four-day hike in the desert, carrying all their supplies. Matt noticed that Randy was lugging a heavy car door and asked him why. Randy replied: "So that when I get hot I can roll down the window." ☆

The washer-and-dryer salesperson says to the customer, "Have you decided on a model?"

"I'm not sure," says the customer.

The salesperson says, "That's no problem—just take it for a spin." ☆

What did the sink say to the dirty dishes?

"You're in hot water now!"

What did the milk say to the blender?

"I'm all shook up."

Why was the saucepan always getting in trouble?

It was too hot to handle.

Why did the teapot blush?

He thought the kettle was whistling at him.

Mrs. Gumbo was backing out of her driveway when she heard a thump. She stopped the car in a panic and rushed out to see what had happened. There, at the end of the driveway, was a small dog lying on its side. It was dead. Mrs. Gumbo felt awful. She knew it was her neighbor's dog. Looking very worried, she climbed the front stairs of her neighbor's house and knocked on the door. She waited for a couple of minutes. Finally, a tall man answered.

"I'm so sorry," Mrs. Gumbo said. "I was backing out of my driveway just a few minutes ago when I heard a thump. I got out of the car to see what had happened. Your dog was lying dead at the end of the driveway. I'm afraid that I ran over her and I feel terrible about it. I *insist* on replacing her."

The tall man paused and then said, "Well, I guess you can bring me my slippers and newspaper tomorrow morning." ☆

131

What did the soda say to the bottle opener?

"Hey, can you help me find my pop?"

JANET: Sir, can you please call me a taxi?
VALET: Certainly. You are a taxi.

Why was the pantry so good at telling the future?

It knew what was in store.

What did the broom say to the dustpan?

"Let's make a clean sweep."

Why does the toast like the knife?

Because the knife butters him up.

If a nut on a wall is a walnut, what is a nut in the bathroom?

A pee can.

Funny Fact

Laughter is good for you! Just ask a gelatologist, a scientist who studies laughter. When you laugh, chemicals that make you happy, called "endorphins," are released in your brain. ☆

PEPPER SHAKER: Why won't the salt shaker shake out any salt?
KETCHUP BOTTLE: I suppose it goes against the grain.

What do you get when you cross a bed with a kitchen appliance?

A four-poster toaster.

ha-ha!

140

Truly TASTELESS JOKES

Food Strikes Back

What do you call cheese that isn't yours?

Nacho cheese.

LITTLE GIRL: I'm thirsty.
LITTLE BOY: I'm Friday. Come over Saturday and we'll have a sundae.

CUSTOMER: Do you serve crabs here?

WAITER: We serve everyone. Sit right down.

I'LL have the fish.

Would you like seaweed with that?

Did you hear about the farmer arrested for selling rotten fruit?

He was judged by his pears.

Why did the cucumber need a lawyer?

It was in a pickle.

Did you ever wonder . . .

. . . what was the best thing before sliced bread?

142

PRACTICAL JOKE

Ways to torment the pizza guy:

Ask for the crust on top this time.

Ask if you get to keep the pizza box when you're done. When they say yes, act very relieved.

Pretend you know the person on the phone from somewhere. Say something like, "Hey, your voice sounds familiar. . . I think we went to bed-wetters camp together about five years ago!"

Make the first topping you order pepperoni. Just before you hang up, say, "Remember—no pepperoni, please!" Don't wait for a response.

If the person on the other end gets annoyed with you, say, "The last guy let me do it!"

PIZZA

Why do nuns like Swiss cheese the best?

Because it's hole-y.

Why did the cookie go to the hospital?

Because it felt crummy.

There are two muffins sitting in a microwave. The first muffin turns to the second and says, "Wow, it's hot in here."

The second replies, "Oh my gosh, a talking muffin!" ☆

What did one raspberry say to the other?

"Look at the jam you got us into!"

143

If you eat three-quarters of a pie, what do you have?

An angry parent!

Why didn't the prawn share his dessert?

He was shellfish.

Why is monastery food so greasy?

It's all cooked by friars.

What did the mama melon say to her daughter when the girl wanted to run away and marry her boyfriend?

"You canteloupe."

Did you hear the one about the compulsive liar sandwich?

It was full of baloney.

What goes best with toast when you're in a car?
Traffic jam.

What's big and white and lives on Mars?

A martian-mallow.

Why are raspberries such bad drivers?
They're always getting into jams.

144

What did the cucumber say to the vinegar?
"Well, this is a fine pickle you've gotten us into!"

Why was the mushroom the hit of the party?
He was a fungi.

What do you get when you cross a cow with an earthquake?
Milkshakes.

How did the vegetable feel after it was cooked?
It was steamed.

BART: I feel like spaghetti.
HOWARD: Funny, you don't look like spaghetti!

What is the heaviest kind of soup?
Won-ton soup!

Adam Sandler

Adam Sandler is a multitalented comedian whose zany onstage persona recalls that of his comic heroes Rodney Dangerfield and Cheech and Chong. In reality, however, Sandler doesn't drink, doesn't do drugs, and is so close to his parents that he called one of his comedy albums *Stan and Judy's Kid* in their honor.

Sandler was first noticed during his five-year stint on *Saturday Night Live,* the popular comedy sketch show on NBC. From 1990 to 1995, Sandler portrayed characters like Opera Man. It was on *SNL* that Sandler began writing and performing original songs, like his wildly popular "Chanukah Song," "Lunchlady Land," and "Red Hooded Sweatshirt." These and other songs appear on Sandler's four comedy albums.

It wasn't long before Hollywood began calling Sandler's name. Sandler had appeared in a few feature films while on *SNL,* but it was his portrayal of a goofy kid forced to repeat all twelve grades in order to receive his inheritance in 1995's *Billy Madison* that cemented his name in moviegoers' minds. Sandler followed with a role as a hockey-player-turned-golfer in *Happy Gilmore* (1996) and fans saw the softer side of Sandler in *The Wedding Singer* (1998) and *Click* (2006), where he is given a remote that can pause and fast-forward parts of his life. Sandler also lent his voice to the character of Count Dracula in *Hotel Transylvania* (2012) and its sequel (2015).

Incidentally, the same group of New York University buddies who helped Sandler write the comedy routines that he performed in New York and Boston clubs and on the college circuit now help him write his movies!

Sandler's multimedia success is proof of a winning combination of wackiness and warm fuzziness.

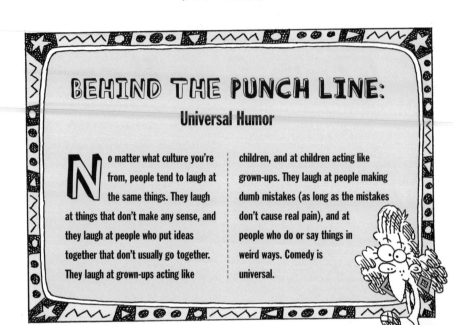

BEHIND THE PUNCH LINE:
Universal Humor

No matter what culture you're from, people tend to laugh at the same things. They laugh at things that don't make any sense, and they laugh at people who put ideas together that don't usually go together. They laugh at grown-ups acting like children, and at children acting like grown-ups. They laugh at people making dumb mistakes (as long as the mistakes don't cause real pain), and at people who do or say things in weird ways. Comedy is universal.

LUCY: Would you care to join me in a cup of tea?
LARRY: Do you really think there's enough room for the two of us?

A woman sits down in a restaurant and says to the waiter, "Waiter, I'd like an alligator, and make it snappy."

Robbie and his friends were talking after school. "Where's your favorite place to eat a hamburger?" asked Owen. Jimmy said he liked to sit in the park. Sam said he liked the picnic tables at the fair. "What about you, Robbie?" Owen asked. "Where's your favorite place to eat a hamburger?" Robbie replied, "In my mouth." ☆

Do you have a head of lettuce?
Then how come your face is so green?

CUSTOMER: This food tastes funny.
WAITER: Then why aren't you laughing?

———

CUSTOMER: Waiter, there's a jack in my soup!
WAITER: That's because we made it with bean stock.

———

CUSTOMER: This coffee tastes like dirt.
WAITER: Yes, that's because it was only ground 20 minutes ago.

———

CUSTOMER: Waiter, there's a fly in my soup!
WAITER: Don't worry, sir, I'm sure he won't drink much.

———

CUSTOMER: Waiter, there's a fly in my alphabet soup!
WAITER: That's no fly, that's a spelling bee.

———

CUSTOMER: Waiter, there's a fly in my soup!
WAITER: Don't worry, sir, we won't charge you extra for it.

———

CUSTOMER: Waiter, what's this fly doing in my soup?
WAITER: Looks like he's drowning, ma'am.

———

CUSTOMER: Waiter, there's a fly doing the breaststroke in my soup!
WAITER: You're mistaken, sir. That's the butterfly.

———

CUSTOMER: Yesterday there was a fly in my soup, but today there's a bee!
WAITER: That's because it's the fly's day off, sir.

Look—we know it was YOU! Your sesame seeds were found at the scene!

Why do blue cheeses look alike?

They're all cut from the same mold.

How do you know carrots are good for your eyes?

Because you never see rabbits wearing glasses.

What did the police do with the hamburger?

They grilled him.

148

Why did the woman divorce the grape?

She was tired of raisin' kids.

What did the grape say when the rhinoceros trampled it?

Not much. It just let out a little wine.

Why did the insect collector toss the butter dish across the restaurant?

He wanted to see the butter fly.

What did the TV dinner say after it had been packaged?

"Curses, foiled again!"

Why did the sandwiches leave the bar?

Because it didn't serve food.

Why was the man staring at the can of orange juice?

Because it said concentrate.

Why did the egg accuse the chef of cruelty?

He put her in a bowl and beat her.

Will Smith

Will Smith is one versatile comic! He's enjoyed success in movies, on TV, and in the music industry. Smith started his career as a member of the rap duo DJ Jazzy Jeff and the Fresh Prince. (In school, Smith was given the nickname "Prince" because of his uncanny ability to charm his way out of trouble.) His duo eventually won a Grammy award for their humorous songs such as "Parents Just Don't Understand," featuring lyrics that any kid could appreciate!

When television producers noticed Smith's ability to perform, they offered him a television show. The sitcom *The Fresh Prince of Bel-Air* ran from 1990 to 1996 and centered on a boy called Will (named for the talented star!) who moved away from his troubled home in Philadelphia to live with rich relatives in Bel-Air, California. Smith wrote the rap theme to the series. The show and its theme song remain among the best-known pop culture artifacts of the '90s.

After conquering the TV comedy world, Smith moved on to films. He starred in the *Men in Black* movies (1997, 2002, 2012), which center around spoofs on aliens visiting Earth. Other comedy movies include *Shark Tale* (2004), an animated film about a fish who saves his reef community only to find himself "in over his head" with a gang of underwater sea creatures; and *Hitch* (2005), where he plays a professional "date doctor." Though he opts for more serious roles nowadays, he still brings humor to each character.

Smith has proved his talent in music, TV, and film. Is there any comedic territory he hasn't covered?

What kind of exercises do pancakes do?

Jumping flapjacks.

Where do lettuces practice law?

At the salad bar.

How do you make a casserole?

Put it on a skateboard.

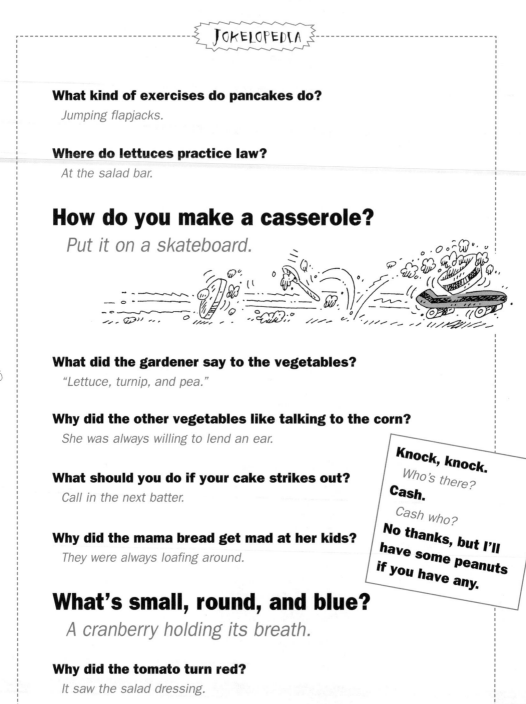

What did the gardener say to the vegetables?

"Lettuce, turnip, and pea."

Why did the other vegetables like talking to the corn?

She was always willing to lend an ear.

What should you do if your cake strikes out?

Call in the next batter.

Why did the mama bread get mad at her kids?

They were always loafing around.

What's small, round, and blue?

A cranberry holding its breath.

Why did the tomato turn red?

It saw the salad dressing.

Knock, knock.
Who's there?
Cash.
Cash who?
No thanks, but I'll have some peanuts if you have any.

156

What do you call two banana peels?

A pair of slippers.

What do you get when you cross an ear of corn with a spider?

Cob webs.

What did the corn give his fiancée when he proposed?

An ear ring.

151

A broccoli, a tomato, and a yam were running in a race. The broccoli got off to a great start, but being a green runner, didn't have the strength to finish the race. The yam and the tomato were neck and neck for the first stretch, but the tomato quickly fell behind. The yam was about to reach the end of the track, but collapsed in exhaustion right before the finish line. Over the course of an hour, the tomato ran the entire length of the race, and won.

Why was the tomato so successful?

The tomato paste itself. ☆

What do you get when you cross a bee with some beef?

A humburger.

A Zen master walks into a pizza parlor and says,

"Make me one with everything."

Why didn't the salad joke make it into the book?

It got tossed.

MARIA: My brother is on a seafood diet.
SHELLY: What's that?
MARIA: He eats whenever he sees food.

ha-ha!

HUSBAND: Why can't you make bread like your mother?
WIFE: I would if you made dough like your father!

What's worse than finding a worm in the apple you're eating?

Finding half a worm!

What does a millionaire make for dinner every night of the week?

Reservations.

Why couldn't the monkey catch the banana?

The banana split.

How do you keep your dog from begging at the table?

Let him taste your cooking.

Why did the doughnut make a dentist's appointment?

Because it needed a filling!

Try this everyday play on words.

Say your brother asks you to make him a peanut butter sandwich. What do you say? Pretend you're a genie who has the power to transform!

YOUR BROTHER: Could you make me a peanut butter sandwich?
YOU: Abracadabra! There, you're a peanut butter sandwich.

The same gag works for other types of sandwiches, chocolate cakes, and cups of tea. This joke is good for a few laughs, but don't do it too often or someone might start playing tricks on you!

SHOWBIZ SHENANIGANS

Games with Famous Names

Which movie director always forgets to wear sunblock?
Steven Peelberg.

What gets Jackie Chan sick every winter?
Kung flu.

What did Bugs Bunny say to Michael Jordan?

"Eh . . . what's up, jock?"

Who is Superman's most religious enemy?
Lex Lutheran.

How do you make Lady Gaga mad?
Poker face.

Eh...what's up, jock?

ary Poppins moved to California and started a business telling people's fortunes. But she didn't read palms or tea leaves, she smelled a person's breath. The sign outside read: "Super California Mystic, Expert Halitosis." ☆

n hour after dropping off her film at the 1-hour photo counter, Snow White rushed back, excited to pick up the developed pictures.

"Sorry," said the clerk, "our machine got jammed. Your pictures won't be ready today."

"But I really need them soon—when do you expect them?" asked a very distressed Snow White.

"Don't worry," the clerk said with a smile. "Someday your prints will come." ☆

154

What does Ariel like on her toast?

Mermalade.

kipper was always bragging to his boss, "You know, I know everyone there is to know. Just name someone, anyone, and I know them." One day, tired of Skipper's boasting, his boss calls his bluff. "Okay, Skipper, how about Tom Cruise?"

"Sure, yes, Tom and I are old friends, and I can prove it." So Skipper and his boss fly out to Hollywood and knock on Tom Cruise's door, and sure enough, Tom Cruise shouts, "Skipper! Great to see you! You and your friend come right in and join me for lunch!"

Although impressed, Skipper's boss is still skeptical. After they leave Cruise's house, he tells Skipper that he thinks it was just lucky that Skipper knew Cruise.

"Go ahead, name anyone else," Skipper says.

"The president of the United States," his boss quickly replies.

"Yes," Skipper says, "I know him. Let's fly out to Washington." And off they go. As they tour the White House, the president spots Skipper and motions him and his boss over, saying, "Skipper, what a surprise! I was just on my way to a meeting, but you and your friend come on in and let's have a cup of coffee first and catch up." Well, the boss is very shaken by now, but still not totally convinced. After they leave the White House grounds, he expresses his doubts to Skipper, who again tells him to name anyone else.

"The Pope," his boss suggests.

"Sure!" says Skipper. "My family is very religious, and I've known the Pope a long time." So off they fly to Rome. Skipper and his boss are assembled with the masses in Vatican Square when Skipper says, "This will never work. I can't catch the Pope's eye among all these people. Tell you what—I know all the guards, so let me just go upstairs and I'll come out on the balcony with the Pope." And he disappears into the crowd headed toward the Vatican. Sure enough, half an hour later Skipper emerges with the Pope on the balcony. But when Skipper returns, he finds that his boss has had a heart attack and is surrounded by paramedics. Making his way to his boss's side, Skipper asks him, "What happened?"

His boss looks up and says, "I was doing fine until you and the Pope came out on the balcony and the man next to me said, 'Who's that on the balcony with Skipper?'" ☆

A car was traveling down the road at 90 miles per hour when it passed a police officer. After pulling the car over, he called the station to report a speeding car with a VIP inside it. The chief asked, "Who's in the car, the mayor?"

The officer told him, "No, someone more important than the mayor."

Then the chief asked, "Is it the governor?"

The officer answered, "No, someone more important than the governor."

The chief finally asked, "Is it the president?"

The officer answered once again, "No, someone even more important than the president."

This made the chief very curious, so he asked, "Now who is more important than the president?"

"I'm not really sure, chief," the officer replied. "But he must be important because he has the Pope as his chauffeur." ☆

156

Darn! Not again!

Gesundheit!

What stands in New York, holds a torch, and sneezes a lot?
The Ah-Choo of Liberty.

What kind of car does Luke Skywalker drive?
A To-yoda.

What did Michael Jackson say to bullies?
"Beat it."

What do you call a little blue man who lives on the West Coast?
Papa Surf.

What do you call a gorilla with a green thumb?
Hairy Potter.

How did Minnie Mouse save Mickey from drowning?

She gave him mouse-to-mouse resuscitation.

How do you make a Rolling Stone?

Push a rock down a hill.

What did the Lone Ranger say after he was thrown from his horse?

"I've fallen and I can't giddyup."

Bill Gates, Michael Jordan, a Zen master, and a delivery man were all traveling together on a plane. Suddenly, they found themselves in a terrible storm. After several minutes of turbulence, the pilot went running back to them and announced that lightning had hit the plane, and they were going to crash in a matter of minutes. "There are only four parachutes, so one of us will be left out," he announced. "Since I'm the pilot, I get one!" Before anyone could argue, the pilot grabbed a parachute and jumped out of the plane.

"I'm the world's greatest athlete," proclaimed Michael Jordan. "The world needs great athletes, so I must live." He then grabbed a parachute and leaped out of the plane.

"I'm the smartest man in the world," bragged Bill Gates. "The world needs smart men, so I must also live!" He grabbed the third parachute and jumped out of the plane.

At this point, the Zen master began to speak. "I have lived a long life compared to you, so you must take the last parachute. I will go down with the plane."

"You don't have to!" said the delivery man. "The world's smartest man jumped out of the plane with my backpack." ☆

157

What do you call a breakfast sandwich with mussels?

The Arnold Shellfish 'n' egger.

What do you get when you cross a puppet who lives in a garbage can with a kangaroo?

Oscar the Pouch.

What do you call a super pig who can climb up the side of buildings?

Spiderham.

Would Little Miss Muffet share her curds?

No whey.

158

> Don't diss me like this, Muffy-baby!

What would you get if you crossed a great hockey player with a Sea-Doo?

Wayne Jet-Ski.

What did Huey, Dewey, and Louie say when something was falling on their uncle's head?

"Donald—duck!"

Where did the Arabian knights live?

In sand castles.

What do you get when you cross a serial killer with a pair of jeans?

Jack the Zipper.

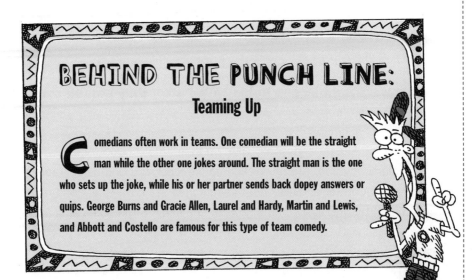

BEHIND THE PUNCH LINE:
Teaming Up

Comedians often work in teams. One comedian will be the straight man while the other one jokes around. The straight man is the one who sets up the joke, while his or her partner sends back dopey answers or quips. George Burns and Gracie Allen, Laurel and Hardy, Martin and Lewis, and Abbott and Costello are famous for this type of team comedy.

What is Homer Simpson's favorite ice cream?
Chocolate chip cookie d'oh.

What's green and sings?
Elvis Parsley.

How do you know Dorothy was a good actress?
She brought the house down.

Why couldn't the Tin Man join in the card game?
They were playing Hearts.

What did Dorothy do when her dog got stuck?
She called a Toto truck.

Who's a lamb's favorite superhero?

B-a-a-atman.

What were Batman and Robin called after they got run over?

Flatman and Ribbon.

Grumpy, Sleepy, and Dopey were on their lunch break at the diamond mine. Grumpy picked up his lunch box and said, "I really hate peanut butter and liverwurst sandwiches. If I have to eat one more peanut butter and liverwurst sandwich, I'm going to run screaming into the woods." And Sleepy said, "I know what you mean. Every day I open my lunch box and it's the same old thing: salami and ketchup. I'm so tired of salami and ketchup sandwiches. If I have one again today, I'm going to go jump in the river." And Dopey said, "Gee, I have a broccoli and mustard sandwich every day. If that's what's in my lunch today, I'll run straight up that hill and stay there." So all three dwarfs carefully opened their lunch boxes and discovered the same thing they ate every day. Grumpy flipped out and ran screaming into the woods, Sleepy jumped in the river, and Dopey ran off up the hill. That evening, the other four dwarfs told Snow White what had happened at lunchtime. "Grumpy and Sleepy always whine about the lunches I make for them, but I don't understand what got into Dopey," said a puzzled Snow White. "He makes his own lunch!" ☆

What do you call a famous pirate who always skips school?

Captain Hooky.

What did the chicken say to Arnold Schwarzenegger?

"I'll be bock . . . bock, bock."

I'll be bock... bock, bock.

Gilligan's Island

What do you get when you take a cruise ship, seven passengers, and a terrible storm that shipwrecks them on a deserted island? *Gilligan's Island,* the hit sitcom that ran from 1964 to 1967. The bumbling but well-meaning Gilligan, the ship's grumpy Skipper, a millionaire couple, a movie star named Ginger, the wise Professor, and a farm girl called Mary Ann are seven castaways who live an island lifestyle so hilarious that you'll want to be stranded with them! Tune in to a rerun, or to one of the two cartoons or three TV-movie spinoffs to find out if they ever manage to escape the island. . .

161

Why was Cinderella thrown off the baseball team?

She kept running away from the ball.

What do you get when you cross Cinderella with a barber?

Glass clippers.

What do you get when you cross a rabbit with Cinderella?

A hare ball.

What Greek king was purple and conquered the ancient world?

Alexander the Grape.

Who's young and perky and attacks sports officials?

Buffy the Umpire Slayer.

Goldilocks was walking along one sunny afternoon when she found a beautiful house in the woods. The door was open, so she walked right in. There she found a table set with three bowls of steaming porridge. "Hello?" she called out, but no one was home. She tried the first bowl, but it was too hot. She tried the second bowl, but it was too cold. Then she tried the third bowl, and it was just right. "Wow," she said, once she had finished the meal. "Now I'm feeling very sleepy." So she wandered around looking for a bed. She couldn't find one anywhere on the bottom floor. Finally, she found a staircase at one end of the house. She climbed up the steps and went into the first room. There was a great big bed in the middle of the room, so Goldilocks jumped right in. "Yikes!" she exclaimed. "This one's too hard!" She wandered into the next room. There she found another bed, and hopped right in it. But it was too soft. By this time, Goldilocks was very tired. She went into the third room, and yelled out in surprise. There were three pink pigs cowering in the corner of the room. "Wait a second," she said. "You guys are in the wrong fairy tale."

"No, we're not," answered one of the pigs. "Don't you know this is a two-story house?" ✪

162

What do Tarzan and Jane sing at Christmastime?

Jungle Bells.

Yes...feel the Force, Young Skywhopper! Now, ketchup you will need...

What do you get when you cross Darth Vader's son with a hamburger?

The Luke Skywhopper.

The Three Stooges

The Three Stooges were the ultimate slapstick comedians. Just picture three big men trying to fit through a tiny door all at once, and you'll have a good mental image of the Stooges.

The Howard brothers, Moses (Moe), Shemp, and Larry Fine were the original Stooges. They performed in vaudeville shows during the 1920s and 1930s before becoming movie stars. Jerome Howard (Curly) replaced Shemp in 1932. Actor Ted Healy, who played their straight man in films for many years, explained the concept behind the name. "A stooge is a guess-man. You can never guess what he's going to do next." The Three Stooges were great because they were so unpredictable. Even their classic poke-in-the-eye, slap-in-the-face, punch-in-the-belly routine had funny variations and consequences.

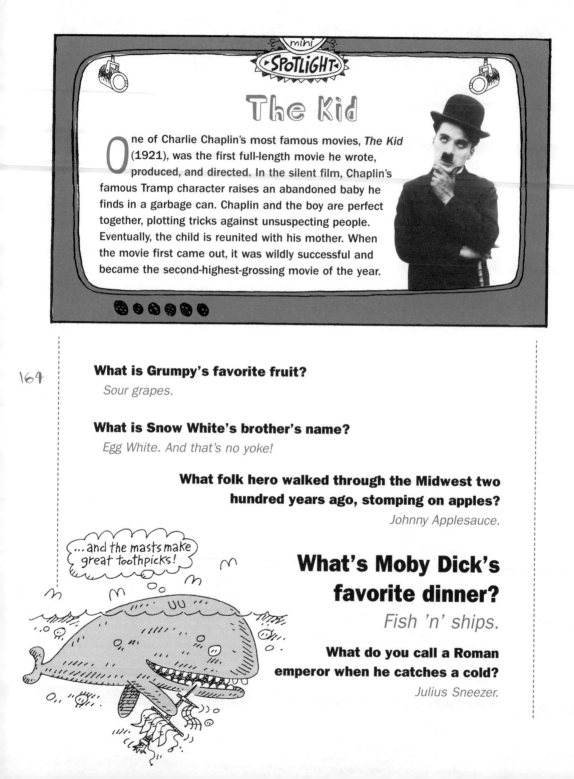

Mini SPOTLIGHT

The Kid

One of Charlie Chaplin's most famous movies, *The Kid* (1921), was the first full-length movie he wrote, produced, and directed. In the silent film, Chaplin's famous Tramp character raises an abandoned baby he finds in a garbage can. Chaplin and the boy are perfect together, plotting tricks against unsuspecting people. Eventually, the child is reunited with his mother. When the movie first came out, it was wildly successful and became the second-highest-grossing movie of the year.

What is Grumpy's favorite fruit?

Sour grapes.

What is Snow White's brother's name?

Egg White. And that's no yoke!

What folk hero walked through the Midwest two hundred years ago, stomping on apples?

Johnny Applesauce.

...and the masts make great toothpicks!

What's Moby Dick's favorite dinner?

Fish 'n' ships.

What do you call a Roman emperor when he catches a cold?

Julius Sneezer.

What's black and white and black and white?

101 Dalmatians.

Will Ferrell

Will Ferrell became interested in comedy in high school, where he volunteered on the daily public address and gave morning announcements in silly disguised voices. That's when he first realized that he loved to make people laugh.

Unlike many funny performers, Ferrell does not have a background in stand-up comedy. Originally, he wanted to become a sports broadcaster. He even received a degree in sports broadcasting from the University of Southern California. When a joke he made on-air in one of his classes drew laughter, Ferrell decided to make the dive into full-time acting.

He became involved in improvisational comedy, where performers talk and act spontaneously, usually in response to what an audience member suggests. His career began to fly when he was picked up by *Saturday Night Live*, the long-running, sketch comedy show.

On *SNL*, Ferrell's genius was his ability to portray honest characters in absurd situations. He imitated everyone from presidents Bill Clinton and George W. Bush to *Jeopardy!* host Alex Trebek. Some of the best characters he played were the ones he created himself! In those roles he was well known as Craig Buchanan, a super enthusiastic cheerleader, and Marty Culp, a middle school music teacher who played educational medleys to the tune of pop music.

After *SNL*, Ferrell made an easy transition to film. His first role in a blockbuster movie came in 2001's *Zoolander*, where he played a fiendish fashion designer (he also starred in the 2016 sequel). He followed this with starring roles in *Elf* (2003), as a human raised by elves at the North Pole; *Anchorman: The Legend of Ron Burgundy* (2004), as a self-obsessed newscaster; and *The Lego Movie* (2014) and *Daddy's Home* (2016).

You'd never guess it, but in spite of the wacky nature of many of his characters, Ferrell claims to be quite shy in person.

SOUNDING A FUNNY NOTE

Bust a Gut in the Band Room

What kind of music do they play at Stonehenge?

Hard rock.

What kind of music do they play at a playground?

Swing.

What kind of music do they play at a soft-drink factory?

Pop.

What kind of music do they play at a construction site?

Heavy metal.

What kind of music do they play at a nacho factory?

Salsa.

What kind of music do mummies listen to?

Rap.

How many drummers does it take to change a lightbulb?

One, two . . . one, two, three, four!

How many country musicians does it take to change a lightbulb?

Five: One to change the bulb, and four to sing about how much they'll miss the old one.

How many folk musicians does it take to change a lightbulb?

Forty: One to change the bulb, and thirty-nine to complain that it's electric.

What happens when you drop a piano down a mine shaft?

A minor B-flat.

What do you get when you drop a piano on an army base?

A major B-flat.

Why didn't the opera singer get a job on the cruise ship?

Because she was afraid of the high Cs.

Uh-Oh...

CLICK!

PRACTICAL JOKES

Beginner Version

Use superglue to attach a quarter to the sidewalk. Watch people try to pick it up. Warning: don't try this on a busy sidewalk or street.

Advanced Version

Attach a dollar to a long piece of fishing line. Pull it along a sidewalk and watch people try to grab it. If someone comes close, jerk the fishing line and pull it out of his or her reach while you hide.

169

One night a woman is walking through a graveyard in Vienna when all of a sudden she hears music. No one is around, so she starts looking to see where it's coming from. She finally finds the source and notices it's coming from a grave with a headstone that reads "Ludwig van Beethoven."

She then realizes that the music is one of Beethoven's famous symphonies, but that it is being played backward. Puzzled, she leaves the graveyard and convinces a friend to return with her. By the time they arrive back at the grave, the music has changed. This time it is a different Beethoven symphony, but the music is still being played backward.

Curious, the ladies agree to consult a classical music expert. When they return with the expert, yet another Beethoven symphony is playing, and the expert agrees that the symphonies are truly being played backward.

By the next day word has spread and a huge group gathers around the grave to hear the symphonies being played backward. Just then the graveyard's caretaker comes up to the crowd. Someone in the group asks him if there is an explanation for the music.

"Oh, it's nothing to worry about," says the caretaker. "Beethoven is just decomposing." ☆

When is a tire a bad singer?
When it's flat.

Why was Mozart mad at his chickens?
They kept saying, "Bach, Bach, Bach."

Why is Homer Simpson bad at singing scales?
He always gets stuck at "Doh!"

What did the drummer say when his band teacher told him he had no rhythm?
"That's because I'm beat."

I'm sure it's just temporary...

How do you catch a percussionist who's on the run?
Use a snare drum.

Why did the boy stop practicing the violin at Christmas?
Because his mother asked for peace on earth.

What's the world's oldest rock group?
The Rolling Flintstones.

Why did the Beatles break up?
They started to bug each other.

The Simpsons

Who would guess that a family of five yellow, bug-eyed, four-fingered people with bad overbites and weird hairdos would ever see the light of day on television—much less keep a show going for over 20 years?

Guess again. The Simpson family—parents Homer and Marge and kids Bart, Lisa, and Maggie—are the stars of *The Simpsons,* a cartoon show that has made history. Created by a cartoonist named Matt Groening, the show is both wickedly funny and very intelligent, appealing to kids and adults alike. Groening has said that keeping the jokes fresh is one of the biggest challenges to keeping a show like *The Simpsons* alive for so long, so he makes sure he always inserts what he calls "freeze-frame gags," which are jokes that require you to watch the show again in freeze-frame motion in order to catch them. Funny guest stars who lend their distinctive voices to the show are another way to keep it fresh. Good writing is the secret to good comedy, and *The Simpsons* is no exception. A crack team of writers ensures that viewers will keep coming back to watch Bart write new messages on his chalkboard and see what happens when the family files in to sit on the couch. *The Simpsons* was made into a movie in 2007, has won more than 25 Primetime Emmy Awards, has been listed by *TV Guide* as one of the "50 Greatest TV Shows of All Time," and was also awarded a star on Hollywood's Walk of Fame. Quirkiness and an ability to keep the jokes coming—these are two signs of greatness in comic television.

Two boys were camping in the backyard. Late at night they started wondering what time it was. "Start singing really loudly," one of them suggested.

"How will that help?" asked the other boy.

"Just do it," insisted the first.

They both started singing as loudly as they could. Moments later, a neighbor threw open her window and shouted, "Keep it down! Don't you know it's three o'clock in the morning?" ☆

What do you get when a rhinoceros steps on your record?
A smashed hit.

What do you get when you cross a bunch of monkeys with an orchestra?
A chimp-phony.

172

Why did the trombone player fall behind in his work?
Because he kept letting things slide.

Why did the piano become a locksmith?
It had lots of keys.

What kind of music do balloons hate?
Pop.

What happened to the house built of cymbals?
The whole thing came crashing down.

THE MAKING OF A COMEDIAN

Step 5: Sequencing and the "Play Frame"

Telling a joke can produce a chuckle, but tell two or three jokes in the proper sequence and you can have your audience rolling on the floor. The classic joke sequence is the "Why did the chicken cross the road?" series, where the punch line or question varies slightly with each telling. This method works really well for two reasons: first, your listener is already warmed up, and wants to keep laughing; second, you're playing off an expectation. The audience expects to hear the classic joke, but instead gets a new, alternate joke. This makes the joke twice as funny. It's like a clown hitting someone in the face with a pie, and then his victim asking for ice cream on the side.

When you've been telling jokes and your giddy friends are laughing, it's easy to keep them going; in psychology, this state is referred to as a "play frame." A play frame is a situation that makes people expect everything to be funny. For instance, if you're watching a sitcom like *Friends*, or reading a joke book, you expect funny things! You're more prepared to laugh than when you're watching the news. This is one reason why "Top Ten" lists work so well: the list is a series of ten jokes, and you're looking forward to laughing at all of them.

173

Why did the sheet music run away from the singer?

She kept hitting all the notes.

Why did the mandolin go to the psychiatrist?

It was tired of being high-strung.

What did the grouchy trumpet say to the trumpeteer?

Can you can a piano?

No, but you can tuna fish.

How do you make a bandstand?

Take away their chairs.

Don't give me any of your lip!

174

What do you call a keyboard with good morals?

An upright piano.

That love look in Your eyes... as you slurp down those flies... it's witchcraft....

What kind of music do long-distance truckers listen to?

Cross-country music.

Why couldn't the concertgoer get her money back when the singer was off-key?

Because she paid the flat rate.

The Name Game

What do you call a man in debt? *Owen.*

What do you call an adventurous man? *Darin.*

What do you call a man who likes loud music? *Blaire.*

What do you call a man who rolls in leaves? *Russell.*

What do you call a man in the middle of a bull ring? *Gord.*

What do you call a man with three eyes? *Seymore.*

What do you call a man who owes money? *Bill.*

A mangy-looking guy goes into a diner and orders a cup of coffee. The waitress says, "No way. I don't think you can pay for it."

The guy says, "You're right. I don't have any money, but if I show you something you haven't seen before, will you give me a cup?"

The waitress says, "Only if what you show me isn't gross."

"Deal!" says the guy, and he reaches into his coat pocket and pulls out a hamster. He puts the hamster on the counter and it runs across the room and up the piano in the corner, jumps on the keyboard, and starts playing. And the hamster is really good.

The waitress says, "You're right. I've never seen anything like that before. That hamster is truly good on the piano." The guy drinks the coffee and asks for another.

"Money or another miracle, or else no coffee," says the waitress.

The guy reaches into his coat again and pulls out a frog. He puts the frog on the counter, and the frog starts to sing. He has a marvelous voice and great pitch. He's a fine singer. A stranger from the other end of the counter rushes over to the guy and offers him $300 for the frog. The guy says, "It's a deal." He takes the money and gives the frog to the stranger.

ha-ha!

The stranger runs out of the diner.

The waitress says to the guy, "Are you some kind of nut? You sold a singing frog for $300? It must be worth millions. You must be crazy."

"Not so," says the guy. "The hamster is also a ventriloquist." ☆

176

Why did the drummer bring a chicken to band practice?

He needed new drumsticks.

ATHLETIC ANTICS

Really Sock It to 'Em in the Gym

What's a good place to take your golf clubs after the game?
A tee party.

Why do pro baseball players spin around a lot?
To get ready for the whirl series.

What's the best thing to drink during a marathon?
Running water.

Are baseball umpires good eaters?
Yes—they always clean their plates.

What did the baseball glove say to the baseball?
"Catch you later."

Why are most baseball games played at night?

Because bats sleep during the day.

How can you tell the difference between a judge and a skating rink?

One is the bringer of justice; the other is just ice.

What position does a pig play in football?

Swinebacker.

178

SALESPERSON: Try this new bandage. You can swim, water-ski, snorkel, or scuba dive with it on!

INJURED CUSTOMER: That's great! I couldn't do any of those things before I hurt myself!

A man and his friend are playing golf at the local golf course one day. The first man is about to putt when he sees a long funeral procession on the road next to the course. He suddenly stops mid-putt, takes off his golf cap, closes his eyes, and bows his head in prayer.

His friend looks at him bewildered and says, "Wow, that is the most thoughtful and touching thing I have ever seen. You truly are a kind man."

The man then replies, "Yeah, well, we were married for 35 years." ☆

Why did the rubber band go to the baseball game?

It wanted to enjoy the seventh-inning stretch.

Why don't eggs make good quarterbacks?

When their defense cracks, they're too quick to scramble.

Why do basketball players stay home during the off-season?

They aren't allowed to travel.

What do you get when you cross a basketball team with cinnamon crullers?

Dunkin' donuts.

How is a basketball player like a baby?

They both dribble!

What has four wheels and grows on a vine?

A skategourd.

Why do scientists love baseball?

They love looking at slides.

Why are tennis games so loud?

Because the players raise a racquet.

When do ballplayers get emotional?

When they choke up on the bat.

Helpful Hints

To help you speed up your morning routine, try the following time-saving tips:

Smear food on your face before bed. When you wake up, lick it off—better than a breakfast bar!

Keep your clothes in the car and get dressed on the way to school.

Shower? Who needs it? Just ask your parents to drive through a car wash with the windows down. But be warned—that big whirling brush really tickles!

Why did the baseball player take her bat to the library?

Her teacher told her to hit the books.

What's black and white and never right?

A hockey referee.

What kind of player gives refunds?

A quarterback!

Why did the athlete take up bowling?

She thought it would be up her alley.

Jimmy and Timmy were playing baseball in their backyard. Jimmy threw a pitch and Timmy connected, hitting the ball over the fence.

After seeing this, Jimmy said, "It's a run home."

"You mean a home run," replied Timmy.

"No, I mean a run home," Jimmy insisted. "You hit the ball through the neighbor's window." ☆

Why couldn't anyone find the deck of cards?

They got lost in the shuffle.

What game do tornadoes like to play?

Twister.

SpongeBob SquarePants

Stephen Hillenburg, marine-biologist-turned-animator, combined his love of underwater creatures and cartoons to create the frenzy of nautical nonsense that is the *SpongeBob SquarePants* cartoon sitcom.

The show's protagonist is a yellow kitchen sponge. SpongeBob SquarePants lives underwater in a two-story pineapple house in Bikini Bottom with his meowing pet snail, Gary. He works as a fry cook at the Krusty Krab fast-food joint. Whether he's bumbling through adventures with his starfish best friend, Patrick, or dodging the pompous Squidward Tentacles, SpongeBob's friendly character always saves the day.

SpongeBob SquarePants appeals to almost everyone, thanks to the humanlike behavior of the Bikini Bottom dwellers. Instead of cars, characters drive boats that have wheels. In fact, Bikini Bottom is like any town . . . only it's under water!

SpongeBob was so popular that Nickelodeon made it into a feature-length film. In the *SpongeBob SquarePants Movie* (2004), the crown of Bikini Bottom's king is stolen. It looks like Mr. Krab, SpongeBob's boss, committed the crime. SpongeBob and Patrick set out to rescue the king and keep him from losing everything, including his life.

SpongeBob cartoons are filled with fun details to watch for. Squidward often makes references to 11 minutes, a nod to the total length of each episode. And in almost every show, someone exclaims, "My leg!" *SpongeBob SquarePants* is so popular because it appeals to kids as well as their parents—the undersea escapades are packed with maximum silliness and genuine optimism.

CALENDAR CUTUPS

It's that time of the year again:
Will February March?
No, but April May.

If April showers bring May flowers,
what do May flowers bring?
Pilgrims.

What is a bug's favorite sport?
Cricket.

What's the difference between a soccer player and a dog?
The soccer player wears a whole uniform, the dog just pants.

Why don't matches play baseball?
One strike and they're out.

What do baseball players give their fiancées?
Diamonds.

What do you get when you cross a baseball pitcher with a carpet?
A throw rug.

Where do hair colorists sit when they go to baseball games?
In the bleachers.

182

Why is it a good idea to have a frog on your baseball team?

They're good at catching pop flies.

Thath the lath thime I thry to cath one with my thongue...

Why did the pitcher bring an old pocket watch to his games?

So he could wind up before throwing the ball.

What do you get when you cross a baseball player with a monster?

A double-header.

Why did the batter tear off his clothes after he hit a home run?

He wanted his team to have a winning streak.

Do old bikers ever die?

No, they just get recycled.

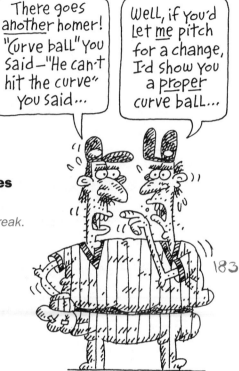

There goes another homer! "Curve ball" you said—"He can't hit the curve" you said...

Well, if you'd let me pitch for a change, I'd show you a proper curve ball...

183

Why is it so windy at sporting events?

Because of all the fans.

Why did the golfer bring two pairs of socks to the tournament?

In case she got a hole in one.

What do you get when you cross a library with a golfer?

Book clubs.

Why was the prizefighter fired from his job?

He was always punching out early.

What do you get when you cross a Chevy with a golf club?

A backseat driver.

Why are a golfer's pants never wrinkled?

Because golfers use nine-irons.

How did the trampolinist beat the prizefighter?

Every time she was knocked down, she bounced right back.

184

Why did the fight fans keep getting punched?

Because they were sitting in the box seats!

Why does it take longer to run from second base to third base than it does from first to second?

Because there's a shortstop between second and third.

What is a boxer's favorite drink?

Fruit punch.

How do gymnasts feel during a routine?

Head over heels.

BEHIND THE PUNCH LINE:
One-Person Shows

A *one-person show* is, as its name suggests, a comedy show performed by only one actor. Such shows are usually done either as a monologue or as a series of skits. A monologue is a long comic piece that is spoken without breaks. Skits are shorter pieces, performed with breaks in between. An actor who is skilled at impersonation or wishes to portray several different characters as part of her show will often use skits. Actors looking for a more dramatic presentation will go for the monologue.

One-person shows are difficult because the focus is all on one actor, who often is the writer, director, and producer of the show as well. But for an actor who wants to focus on one topic that means a lot to her— for example, race or ethnic heritage, or a particular problem she has overcome in her life—it can be a good way to express herself.

185

What game does Godzilla like best?

Squash.

What's a Chrysler's favorite game?

Dodge ball.

What's a diver's favorite game?

Pool.

What kind of match doesn't light on fire?

A tennis match.

Hey-You with the ball in the pouch! That's traveling!

Uh-oh....

Why did the kangaroo lose the basketball game?

He ran out of bounds.

Two 90-year-old men, Moe and Sam, have been friends all their lives. Sam is dying, so Moe comes to visit him. "Sam," says Moe, "you know how we both loved baseball all our lives. You have to do me one favor. When you go, somehow you've got to tell me if there's baseball in heaven."

Sam looks up at Moe from his deathbed and says, "Moe, you've been my friend for many years. I'll do that for you." And with that, he passes on.

At midnight a couple of nights later, Moe is sound asleep when a distant voice calls out to him, "Moe. . . . Moe. . . ."

"Who is it?" asks Moe, sitting up suddenly. "Who is it?"

"Moe, it's Sam."

"Sam? Is that you? Where are you?"

"I'm in heaven," says Sam, "and I've got to tell you, I've got some good news and some bad news."

"Tell me the good news first," says Moe.

"The good news," says Sam, "is that there is baseball in heaven."

"Really?" says Moe. "That's wonderful! What's the bad news?"

"You're pitching Tuesday!" ☆

WHOA! Pop flies are a cinch up here!

FUNNY BUSINESS

Humor at Work

How many carpenters does it take to screw in a lightbulb?

None. That's the electrician's job!

How many jugglers does it take to screw in a lightbulb?

One, but he uses at least three bulbs.

Where do butchers dance?

At the meat ball.

What's a gambler's favorite game show?

The Dice Is Right.

How do garbagemen break up with their girlfriends?

They just dump 'em.

> Why did the Tiger eat the tightrope walker?

> He wanted a well-balanced meal.

A local business was looking for office help. The owners put a sign in the window that read: "Help wanted. Must be able to type, must be good with a computer, and must be bilingual. We are an Equal Opportunity Employer." A short time later, a dog trotted up to the window, saw the sign, and went inside. He looked at the receptionist and wagged his tail, then walked over to the sign, looked at it, and whined. The receptionist got the idea and told the office manager. The office manager looked at the dog and was surprised, to say the least. However, the dog looked determined, so the manager led him into his office. Inside, the dog jumped up on a chair and stared at the manager. The manager said, "I can't hire you. The sign says you have to be able to type." The dog jumped down, went to the typewriter, and typed out a perfect letter. He took out the page and trotted over to the manager and gave it to him, and then jumped back on the chair. The manager was stunned, but then told the dog, "The sign says you have to be good with a computer." The dog went to the computer and created a program that ran perfectly the first time. By now, the manager was totally dumbfounded! He looked at the dog and said, "I realize that you are a very intelligent dog and have some interesting skills. However, I *still* can't give you the job." The dog jumped down, went to a copy of the sign, and put his paw on the sentence that read "We are an Equal Opportunity Employer." The manager said, "Yes, but the sign also says that you must speak two languages." The dog looked calmly at the manager and said, "Meow." ☆

PRACTICAL JOKE

How to freak out people in a crowded elevator:

- Make explosion noises whenever someone hits a button.
- Stand silently in a corner, facing the wall. There is scientific proof that if you do this long enough, the other passengers will all turn and face the wall, too.
- Meow occasionally.
- Bet the other passengers that you can fit a quarter in your nose.
- Yell "Ding!" at each floor.

Who gets the most respect in the circus?

The tall man—everyone looks up to him.

Did you hear that the fire-eater got engaged?

He ran into an old flame.

Did you hear how hard it is to get a job as a sword-swallower?

There's cutthroat competition.

A man who had been working for the circus for many years as Mr. Tiny, the shortest man alive, agreed to meet with a local newspaper reporter one Sunday to be interviewed. The reporter arrived on time but was surprised to be greeted by a man who was nearly six feet tall. The reporter thought he must be in the wrong place and asked for Mr. Tiny.

"That's me," said the man.

"But you're supposed to be short!" said the reporter.

Mr. Tiny said, "I told you—this is my day off." ☆

190

Why did the pantyhose need a lawyer?
They were on the run.

Why did the sticker need a lawyer?
It was ripped off.

ha-ha!

What are a gas station attendant's favorite shoes?
Pumps.

What are a plumber's favorite shoes?
Clogs.

If athletes get athlete's foot, what do astronauts get?
Missile toe.

Maya Rudolph

Like many famous comedians before her, Maya Rudolph got her start as a cast member on *Saturday Night Live*, joining in 2000 after a brief stint with the Groundlings improv troupe. Her command of different accents and a talent for impressions allowed her to play a wide range of characters. The daughter of a soul singer, Maya inherited her mother's musical talent and often sang in sketches on the show.

But the role that really made her a household name came in 2011's blockbuster *Bridesmaids*. The movie, starring *SNL* castmate Kristen Wiig, is about the high jinks and obstacles leading up to Rudolph's character's wedding. The movie was both critically and commercially successful and was one of the first comedies to be nominated for an Academy Award for Best Original Screenplay.

After leaving *SNL*, Rudolph went on to star in the comedy series *Up All Night* and had her own variety show special in 2014. With her ability to play a wide range of characters, we feel this star will be around for a while.

A frog went to a bank to apply for a loan. Patty Whack, the woman in charge of loans, asked if he had anything to leave for collateral. "Don't worry," she said. "When you pay back the loan, we'll return it to you."

He showed her a small porcelain statue and said, "This is what I have. It is a family heirloom and it's very special to me. If it helps my case, I should add that my father is Mick Jagger."

She took the statue to the bank president and said, "There's a frog out there who wants a loan. His dad is Mick Jagger, and this is what he gave me as proof that we can trust him, but I don't know what it is. Should I give him the money?"

The bank president said, "Why, that's a knickknack, Patty Whack, give that frog a loan, his old man's a Rolling Stone." ☆

192

What do you call a king's sore throat?
A royal pain in the neck.

Did you hear about the wizard who became a film director?
He really made movie magic.

How does the snake charmer sign his letters?
"Love and hisses."

Where do spies do their shopping?
At the snooper market.

How did the fisherman go deaf?
He lost his herring.

A young man at a construction site always bragged that he was stronger than everyone else there. He especially made fun of one of the older workers. After a while, the older worker had had enough. "Why don't you put your money where your mouth is?" he said. "I'll bet a week's pay that I can haul something in a wheelbarrow over to that building that you won't be able to wheel back."

"You're on," the braggart replied. "Let's see what you got."

The old man reached out and grabbed the wheelbarrow by the handles. Then, nodding to the young man, he said with a smile, "All right. Get in." ✰

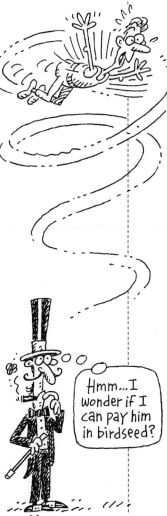

M ortimer the Magnificent tried for ages to get into the circus. When Trevor's Traveling Carnival came to town, he begged and pleaded with the owner to watch his act. The owner finally agreed. Mortimer stepped into the center ring and began flapping his arms wildly, and within moments he rose off the ground. As he went higher and faster, he began to do all kinds of tricks: barrel rolls and loop-the-loops, swan dives and somersaults. After about 20 minutes of this, Mortimer floated back down to the ground and landed gracefully right in front of the circus owner. The owner took a puff on his cigar and asked, "So. What else do you do besides bird impersonations?" ✰

Hmm...I wonder if I can pay him in birdseed?

A private eye had just moved into his new office when there was a knock at the door. He wanted to make a good impression, so he yelled "Come in!" and picked up the phone, pretending to be talking to someone important. The visitor waited patiently, and after a minute the detective hung up the phone and said, "As you can see, I'm very busy. What can I do for you?"

"Not much," replied the visitor. "I'm here to hook up your phone." ☆

194

What do you get when you cross a comedian with crochet?

A knit wit.

Why couldn't the bodybuilder cross the road?

The traffic was too heavy.

A woman is sitting in a park one day, watching two men work. The first man digs a hole, and then the second man fills it back up with dirt. Then the first man digs another hole, and again, the second man fills it back up. They keep doing this over and over again. Finally, the woman asks them, "Why do you keep digging holes and then filling them back in?" One of the guys replies, "Well, usually there's a third guy here who puts in the tree, but he's out sick today." ☆

Why did the comedian put on his sneakers?

He wanted to tell a running joke.

Why did the young woman take the job at the glue factory?

It was fast paste.

The dentist took one look at Billy's mouth and said, "That's the biggest cavity I've ever seen. That's the biggest cavity I've ever seen."

Billy looked at him and said, "I heard you, Doc. You don't have to repeat yourself."

"I didn't. That was an echo." ☆

Why did the upholsterer quit her job?

She was worn out.

Three boys were watching a fire truck roaring down the street with a beautiful Dalmatian riding on top of it.

The first boy said, "They use him to pull children to safety."

"You're wrong," said the second boy. "He helps keep people away from the fire."

"Both of you are wrong," announced the third. "They use him to find the fire hydrant." ☆

196

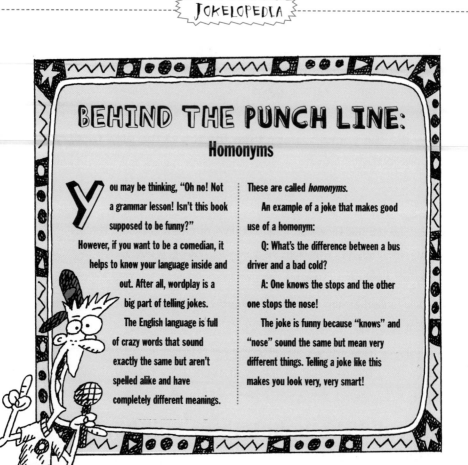

BEHIND THE PUNCH LINE:

Homonyms

You may be thinking, "Oh no! Not a grammar lesson! Isn't this book supposed to be funny?"

However, if you want to be a comedian, it helps to know your language inside and out. After all, wordplay is a big part of telling jokes.

The English language is full of crazy words that sound exactly the same but aren't spelled alike and have completely different meanings.

These are called *homonyms*.

An example of a joke that makes good use of a homonym:

Q: What's the difference between a bus driver and a bad cold?

A: One knows the stops and the other one stops the nose!

The joke is funny because "knows" and "nose" sound the same but mean very different things. Telling a joke like this makes you look very, very smart!

What happened when the dry cleaner was mugged?

He pressed charges.

A young woman is speeding down a freeway when she is stopped by a highway patrol officer. The officer asks if he could please see her driver's license. The woman replies angrily, "I wish you guys would make up your mind. Just yesterday you take away my license, and now you expect me to show it to you!" ☆

A taxi driver picked up his passenger. As they were driving along the passenger tapped the driver on the shoulder to ask him a question. The driver jumped, screamed, lost control of the car, nearly hit a pole, went up on the curb, and stopped inches from a building.

Everything was quiet in the cab, until the driver said, "Please, don't ever do that again. You scared me half to death!"

The passenger apologized and said, "I didn't realize a little tap would scare you that bad."

"Sorry, it's not really your fault," the driver replied. "Today is my first day as a cab driver. Before this I was driving a funeral hearse." ☆

ha-ha!

A young boy enters a barbershop, and the barber turns to his customer and whispers, "This is the dumbest kid in the world. Watch, I'll prove it."

The barber calls the boy over. He then puts a dollar bill in one hand and two quarters in the other and asks the boy, "Which do you want?"

The boy takes the quarters and leaves.

"What did I tell you?" says the barber. "He's been doing that all week. That kid never learns!"

Later, when the customer leaves, he sees the same young boy coming out of the ice-cream store. He walks up to the boy and asks, "Why did you take the quarters instead of the dollar bill?"

The boy licks his cone and replies, "Because the day I take the dollar, the game is over!" ☆

Why are cowboys bad at math?

They're always rounding things up.

Why didn't the cashier get the punch line?

It didn't register.

Why did the boy quit his job at the eraser factory?

His work rubbed him the wrong way.

A woman frantically calls the fire department to report a fire in her neighborhood.

The dispatcher asks, "How do we get there?"

The woman replies, "Don't you still have those big red fire trucks?" ☆

Why did the baker sell his bread only to the rich and famous?

He wanted to work for the upper crust.

What did the baker think of the joke?

He got a rise out of it.

Why did the baker stop making donuts?

He got tired of the hole thing.

Why does Joe work at the bakery?

He kneads the dough.

An astronaut graduated near the bottom of his class. On his first mission into space, he was teamed up with a monkey. They each got an envelope that they were to open once they got into orbit, with instructions for their mission. Once they had blasted off and were in space, the monkey opened his envelope, read the instructions, and began flicking buttons and hitting switches. The astronaut opened up his own envelope and found a note that read:

"Feed the monkey." ☆

Hey-there're bananas in the hold if you want one!

How does the vaudeville player save so much money?
He gets everything for a song and a dance.

Why did the engineer leave locomotive school?
She felt she already had enough training.

Why couldn't the sailors play cards?
Because they were standing on the deck!

Why did the human cannonball choose this line of work?
He wanted to be a big shot.

A woman goes ice fishing. She takes out an ice pick and begins to hack away. She hears a loud voice from above saying, "There're no fish there." She goes to another spot and starts to pick away. Again comes the voice: "There're no fish there either." She tries a third spot. Once more, she hears the voice from above say, "Nope. Not there either." Finally, the woman, growing a little nervous, looks up and asks, "Are you God?" The response from above booms, "No. I'm the arena manager." ☆

What do angels say when they answer the telephone?
"Halo!"

What do you get when you cross a CD player with a secretary?
A stereotype.

Why did the journalist go to the ice-cream parlor?

She wanted to get the scoop.

Why did the coffee-shop waitress love her job?
Because there were so many perks.

What did the farmer say when she fell in the haystack?
"Somebody bale me out!"

What did the tailor say after his client fired him?
"Suit yourself."

A fire started on some grasslands near a farm. The county fire department was called to put out the fire, but it was more than they could handle. Someone suggested calling in the nearby volunteer firefighting crew. Nobody knew if the volunteers would be of any help, but they called them anyway.

The volunteers arrived in a beat-up old fire truck. They rumbled straight toward the fire, drove right into the middle of the flames, and stopped! The volunteer firemen jumped off the truck and started frantically spraying water in all directions. Soon they had snuffed out the center of the fire, breaking the blaze into two smaller parts that they then easily put out.

> I can smell the brakes overheating...

Watching all this, the farmer was so impressed with the volunteer fire department's work and was so grateful that his farm had been spared that right there on the spot he presented the volunteers with a check for $1,000. A local news reporter asked the volunteer fire captain what the department planned to do with the funds.

"That should be obvious," he replied, wiping ashes off his coat. "The first thing we're going to do is get the brakes fixed on our fire truck!" ☆

What has four wheels and flies?

A garbage truck!

Why did the stagehand quit her job?

She wanted a change of scenery.

Why did everyone find the baker funny?

He had a rye sense of humor.

While walking home from work a businessman comes across an old lamp. He gently rubs it and out pops a genie. The genie then informs the man that he may have one wish. The man is incredibly grateful and says, "This is perfect timing. I have a really important presentation to give to the CEO of my company in a couple of days and need it to go smoothly."

"Very well," says the genie. "All you have to do before the presentation is say 'one-two-three' and you'll give the best presentation of your life. However, do not say 'one-two-three-four,' as this will cause you to freeze up and make a fool of yourself. Understand?" The man says he does and continues on his way home.

At home he does what the genie said and tries the presentation and it goes perfectly. He tries it at work the next day and his colleagues give him a standing ovation.

The day of the presentation comes and everything's ready. The CEO signals him to start and he whispers under his breath, "one-two-three."

Then the CEO asks, "What did you say 'one-two-three' for?" ☆

Why did the tailor go to the farm?

So he could sew some oats.

What do farmers plant in their sofas?

Couch potatoes.

When are farmers mean?

When they pull the ears off corn!

A woman is interviewing for a job. The interviewer says, "In this job we need someone who is responsible."

"That's great! I'm definitely the one you want," the woman replies. "At my last job every time something went wrong, they said I was responsible." ☆

203

How do you learn to be a judge?

Mostly through trial and error.

Why was the firefighter lovesick?

She couldn't get over an old flame.

A sailor met a pirate, and they started to talk about their adventures at sea. The sailor noticed that the pirate had a peg leg, a hook, and an eye patch. The sailor asked, "So, how did you end up with the peg leg?"

The pirate replied, "We were in a storm at sea, and I was swept overboard into a school of sharks. Just as my men were pulling me out, a shark bit my leg off."

"Wow!" exclaimed the sailor. "How did you get that hook?"

"Well," replied the pirate, "we boarded an enemy ship and were battling the other sailors with swords. One of them cut off my hand."

"Incredible!" remarked the sailor. "How did you get the eye patch?"

"A seagull dropping fell into my eye," replied the pirate.

"You lost your eye to a seagull dropping?" the sailor asked in surprise.

"Well," said the pirate, "it was my first day with the hook." ☆

204

What kind of trains do ballerinas take?

Tutu trains.

What did the fisherman say to the magician?

"Pick a cod, any cod."

A cowboy traveled from Arizona to Texas on Tuesday, stayed for five days and five nights, and traveled back to Arizona on Tuesday. How was that possible?

His horse was named Tuesday.

Why are perfume salespeople so smart?

They have good scents.

What's the Man of Steel's household chore?

Supper, man.

265

What did the milkmaid say to the anxious butter?

"You'll have to wait your churn."

Does a roller coaster like its work?

It has its ups and downs.

The groundskeeper at a park heard a commotion in the lake. He saw a man thrashing around in the water, and said to him, "Hey, don't you know there's no swimming allowed here?"

"I'm drowning!" screamed the man, trying to keep his head above water.

"Oh well, I guess that's allowed," said the groundskeeper. ☆

SNAP!

PASSENGER: How much to take me to the airport?

CAB DRIVER: Ten dollars, sir.

PASSENGER: And how much for my suitcase?

CAB DRIVER: No charge for the suitcase, sir.

PASSENGER: Okay. Take the case and I'll walk.

FLIGHT ATTENDANT: Would you like dinner, sir?

PASSENGER: What are my choices?

FLIGHT ATTENDANT: Yes or no.

Why do firefighters slide down a pole in the firehouse?

Because it's too hard to slide up.

206

Why do the firemen wear red suspenders?

To keep their pants up.

What did the owner of the coffee shop give to her new employees?

A list of do's and donuts.

Julio's sister asked him what he thought about his job at the plant.

"Well, it's growing on me," said Julio.

Doc-Doc Jokes

You Need a Lot of Patients For This Chapter!

PATIENT: Doctor, doctor, I feel like a pair of curtains. . .
DOCTOR: Then pull yourself together!

NURSE: Doctor, there is an invisible man in the waiting room.
DOCTOR: Tell him I can't see him.

PATIENT: Doctor, I need help. I can never remember what I just said.
DOCTOR: When did you first notice this problem?
PATIENT: Notice what problem?

PATIENT: If the doctor can't see me now, I'm leaving.
NURSE: Calm down. What's wrong with you?
PATIENT: I have a serious wait problem.

This is a difficult diagnosis, Mr. Invisible—nothing seems to show up on any of your tests.

A leopard went to see an eye doctor because he thought he needed a checkup. "What's wrong?" asked the doctor.

"Well, doctor," said the leopard, "every time I look at my wife, I see spots before my eyes."

"What's wrong with that?" asked the doctor. "You are a leopard."

"What's that got to do with anything?" asked the leopard. "My wife's a zebra." ☆

SON: Father, can I ask you a question?
FATHER: Of course.
SON: When a doctor doctors a doctor, does the doctor doing the doctoring doctor as the doctor being doctored wants to be doctored or does the doctor doing the doctoring doctor as he wants to doctor?
FATHER: Uh . . . Ask your mother!

A doctor answers a phone call late one evening and hears the familiar voice of a colleague on the other end of the line. "We need a fourth player for poker," says his friend.

"I'll be right over," says the doctor.

As he is putting on his coat his wife asks, "Where are you going at this hour?"

"I'm sorry, dear," he replies, "but I have an emergency call."

"Is it serious?" asks his wife.

"Oh yes, very serious," replies the doctor gravely. "In fact, there are three doctors there already!" ☆

A man is sitting at home one evening when the doorbell rings. He answers the door to find a six-foot-tall cockroach standing there. The cockroach immediately punches him between the eyes and runs off. The next evening, the man is sitting at home again when the doorbell rings. He answers the door, and the same cockroach is outside. This time, it punches him, kicks him, and karate-chops him before running away. The injured man manages to crawl to the phone and call an ambulance. He is rushed to the hospital where the doctors save his life. The next morning, a doctor asks him what happened. The man explains the attacks by the six-foot-tall cockroach. The doctor thinks for a moment and says, "Yes, I hear there's a nasty bug going around." ☆

WANTED

CONSIDERED SIX-ARMED AND EXTREMELY CRANKY

209

Why did the clown go to the doctor?
He was feeling a little funny.

When do doctors get angry?
When they run out of patients!

Alice said she wasn't feeling well. "You'd better call me a doctor," she said to her friend. Her friend protested, "But I'd rather call you Alice." ☆

What did one elevator say to the other?

I think I'm coming down with something!

PATIENT: Doctor, doctor! You've got to help me!
My hands won't stop shaking!
DOCTOR: Do you drink a lot of coffee?
PATIENT: Not really, I spill most of it!

DOCTOR: I have some bad news and some very bad news.
PATIENT: Okay, give me the bad news first.
DOCTOR: You have 24 hours to live.
PATIENT: Only 24 hours?? That's awful! What could be worse??
DOCTOR: I've been trying to reach you since yesterday.

PATIENT: Doctor, doctor! You've got to help me! Some
mornings I wake up and think I'm Donald Duck. Other
mornings I think I'm Mickey Mouse.
DOCTOR: Hmm, how long have you been having
these Disney spells?

A woman went to her psychiatrist and said,
"Doctor, I want to talk to you about my
husband. He thinks he's a refrigerator."

"That's not so bad," said the doctor.
"It's a rather harmless problem."

"Well, maybe," replied the lady. "But he
sleeps with his mouth open and the light
keeps me awake." ☆

SNORE...

Dr. Seuss

Theodor Geisel was one of the most famous authors ever. Millions of copies of his 40 books, translated into 20 languages, still fill bookshelves all over the world. Chances are, you can recite a passage from a Theodor Geisel book yourself.

You say you have no idea who we're talking about? That's because Theodor Geisel wrote most of his books under a different name (his middle name)—as Dr. Seuss! He added "Dr." because his father always wanted him to become a doctor.

Dr. Seuss's real passion was for creating stories and drawing pictures to go with them. His silly rhymes and goofy illustrations made his work extremely popular with kids and adults alike. Dr. Seuss wrote his first book after reading an article about how boring kids' books were.

Over the course of his long career, Dr. Seuss wrote and illustrated dozens of books, including *The Cat in the Hat, One Fish Two Fish Red Fish Blue Fish,* and *Horton Hears a Who.* His books are not complicated. Once, a book publisher bet him he could not write a book using only 50 words—and he did: *Green Eggs and Ham.* The publisher never paid him! He could only draw one human face, so all of his characters look alike but wear different clothes.

Many of his books have been adapted to the big screen: *How the Grinch Stole Christmas* was made into a cartoon film, as well as a live-action movie starring Jim Carrey in 2000. Mike Myers starred in 2003's *The Cat in the Hat*; Jim Carrey and Steve Carell lent their voices to 2008's *Horton Hears a Who*; and Zac Efron and Taylor Swift voice the main characters in 2012's *The Lorax.* There's even *Seussical,* a Seuss-inspired Broadway musical!

So even though he didn't become a doctor, we should all be glad that Dr. Seuss found his real calling in life—and laughter truly is the best medicine.

A woman went to the doctor complaining of pain. The doctor asked her where it hurt. She replied, "Doctor, everywhere I touch hurts!" The woman touched her shoulder with her finger. "Ouch. That hurts." She took her finger and touched her knee. "Ow, that hurts, too." She then touched her forehead with her finger. "Ouch, it hurts there, too!" She looked at the doctor and asked, "What could it be, doctor?"

The doctor replied, "I know what's wrong with you."

"You do?" replied the woman.

"Yes," said the doctor. "You have a broken finger." ☆

A woman called a psychiatrist and said, "Doctor, my brother thinks he's the Easter Bunny."

"How long has this been going on?" asked the doctor.

"A few years," said the woman.

"Goodness, my dear lady! Why didn't you tell anyone sooner?" asked the doctor.

"Because we needed the eggs." ☆

Why did the doctor go to work for the phone company?

He wanted to be an operator.

A psychiatrist tells her patient, "I've got good news and bad news. The good news is you've got a split personality."

"Are you kidding me?" says the patient. "That's the good news? What's the bad?"

The psychiatrist says, "I'm going to have to bill you twice." ☆

Doc-Doc Jokes

A dermatologist says to her patient, "Look, I have a diagnosis for you: You've got tropical toe rash."

The patient says, "Well, I want a second opinion."

"Okay," says the dermatologist. "You're ugly, too." ☆

A woman goes to her doctor with some concerns about her memory. She tells him that she forgets to pay bills, mail letters, and get groceries, and she can't remember where she's going or what she needs when she gets there. She looks quite worried and asks her doctor, "What can I do?"

The doctor replies, "Pay me in advance." ☆

S even days showed up in the doctor's office.
"What are you doing here?" he asked them.
"Well," they replied, "we're feeling week." ☆

213

mini SPOTLIGHT

iCarly

H ave you ever thought it would be fun to host your own show? *iCarly* shows you just how fun it can be! The series, which ran from 2007 to 2012, follows a girl named Carly Shay (Miranda Cosgrove) and her best friends, Sam and Freddie, as they host their own web show. It all started when, without their knowledge, Freddie filmed Carly and Sam during a school talent show audition and put it online. When the audience demands more, *iCarly* is born. The show, filmed in Carly's loft, is typically full of randomness, craziness, and just pure fun.

THE MAKING OF A COMEDIAN

Step 6: Embellishing

Many of you have probably already mastered this one. Joke telling is just about the only time when lying is a good thing. Lying is allowed, and even necessary in comedy, because jokes are usually made up anyway. We all know that animals don't really talk or drive cars in real life, but they definitely do in the world of comedy.

When you get really good at telling the jokes in this book, try adding stuff on to them. This is called *embellishing*. Add new characters or more pointless situations to the really long and annoying stories in this book and make them even longer and more annoying. In real life, liars embellish to make their stories more believable. In the world of comedy, good joke tellers embellish to make their jokes sillier, dumber, or funnier.

Just remember: The more absurd the lies you tell, the funnier your jokes will be.

A patient went in to see the doctor, and the nurse asked her some questions.

"Name?" asked the nurse.

"Sandra Brown," said the patient.

"Address?" asked the nurse.

"106 Main Street."

"Flu?" asked the nurse.

"No, I walked. It's just around the corner." ☆

A man walks into work with two bandages over his ears. His boss asks what happened. He replies, "I was ironing my shirt when the phone rang. I accidentally answered the iron."

His boss considers this and then asks, "Well, that explains the one ear, but what happened to the other?"

The man replies, "I had to call the doctor!" ☆

A little girl goes to her mom and says, "A boy in my class asked me to play doctor today."

"Oh, dear," the mother says nervously. "What did he have you do?"

"He had me wait over an hour and then told me all I need is rest." ☆

"Doc," said the patient, "my stomach is real bad these days."
"Then send it to bed without supper," said the doctor. ☆

A patient went to the doctor and said, "Doctor, will you give me something for my leg?"

The doctor said, "Well, I don't need it, but I can offer a dollar if you're desperate." ☆

A doctor says to his patient, "Well, I've got good news and bad news. The bad news is, you've got a month to live."

"What? That's awful!" says the patient. "What's the good news?"

The doctor says, "I just won the lottery!" ☆

A patient says to his doctor, "I've thrown my back out again. What should I do?"

The doctor says, "Look through the trash before it's collected!" ☆

A patient goes to see his doctor and says, "Doctor, yesterday I spent all day photographing my nose, and today I can't stop sneezing."

The doctor scratches his chin and asks, "Did you get the pictures back yet?"

"Not yet," says the patient. "Why?"

The doctor says, "Well, obviously, you're developing a cold." ☆

A woman walks into a doctor's office. She has a banana up her nose, a cucumber in her right ear, and a carrot in her left ear. "I don't feel so good, doc," she says. "What's the matter with me?"

The doctor replies, "You're not eating properly." ☆

216

SURGEON: Nurse, did you put the patient to sleep?
NURSE: Yeah, I just told her some of your jokes.

A terrified mother called 911. "Help me!" she said. "My son just swallowed a fork!"

The 911 operator told her not to worry and that he would send an ambulance over right away.

"What should I do until it arrives?" the mother asked him.

The operator said, "Use a spoon." ☆

"*I* 've swallowed a clock!" yells a patient to his doctor. "Please help me, I feel tick to my stomach." ☆

Hmm...doesn't seem to be Tocks-ic...

Tick
Tick
Tick
Tick...

BILL: I've been seeing fuzzy spots in front of my eyes for the past couple of days.
BOB: Did you see a doctor?
BILL: No, just the spots.

MIKE: My brother was sick and went to the doctor.
PAUL: Is he feeling better now?
MIKE: No, he has a broken leg.
PAUL: How did he break it?
MIKE: Well, the doctor gave him a prescription and told him no matter what happened, to follow that prescription. When he got home, the prescription blew out of the window.
PAUL: So how did he break his leg?
MIKE: He jumped out the window trying to follow the prescription.

217

Why did the pie crust go to the dentist?

It needed a filling.

(WARNING: This may be the wurst joke in this book.)

A patient says to his doctor, "I think my throat is wurst."
The doctor says to him, "Ahem—I think you mean 'worse.'"

"No," said the patient. "I mean wurst. Do you know how much it hurts to choke on a sausage?" ☆

A nurse says to a recovering patient, "You're a very lucky man. The doctor took a gallstone the size of a golf ball out of you."

The patient says, "My goodness. I'd like to thank her. Is she around?"

The nurse says, "No, she thought she'd go golfing." ☆

A patient says to his doctor, "I think my tonsils need to be taken out."

The doctor says, "I'll make reservations. Would they prefer dinner or dancing?" ✩

A man made an appointment to see a new optometrist. "Doctor," the man says, "I think I'm suffering from poor eyesight."

"Oh, don't worry," said the doctor. "I can just print your bill bigger." ✩

A patient goes in for surgery on her knee and asks the doctor, "Will I be able to sing?"

Slightly confused, the doctor replies, "The surgery will not affect your vocal cords whatsoever. So you will be able to sing perfectly."

"That's great!" said the patient. "I've always wanted to be able to sing." ✩

COPS AND RIBBERS

A Humorous Twist on the Beat of Life

What do prisoners use to call each other?

Cell phones.

CALLER: Send the fire department, quick! There's a fire in my basement!
911 DISPATCHER: Did you throw water on it?
CALLER: Of course!
911 DISPATCHER: Well, there's no use in their coming then—that's all they ever do.

JUDGE: You look familiar. . . Have we met before?
DEFENDANT: Yes—I taught your daughter to play the drums, remember?
JUDGE: Life in prison for you!

BOY: What happened to the guy who stole your dog?
GIRL: He was charged with pet-ty theft.

DEFENDANT: Your Honor, I'm not guilty of robbery. I'm a locksmith.
JUDGE: Well, what were you doing at the scene of the crime when the police arrived?
DEFENDANT: Just making a bolt for the door!

POLICEMAN: Why did you hit that tree?
DRIVER: Don't blame me! I honked at it but it wouldn't move.

TRAFFIC OFFICER: Did you know this is a one-way street?
DRIVER: Of course—I'm only driving one way!

What do you get when you cross a policeman with an alarm clock?

A crime watch.

What happened to the robber who stole the lamp?

Oh, he got a very light sentence.

What do you call a court case about swimwear?

A bathing suit.

Why was the artist arrested for graffiti?

He had to draw the line somewhere.

How did the robber get caught at the art gallery?

He was framed.

Okay, Van Gogh! Drop the crayons and turn around real slow...

Why did the cops arrest the baseball player?

They heard he had stolen third base.

How was the fish farm robbed?

By hook and by crook.

What do you call it when crooks go surfing?

A crime wave.

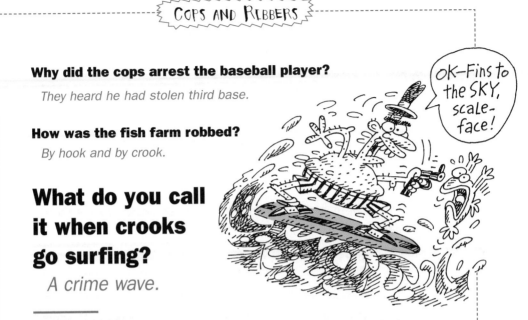

OK—Fins to the SKY, scale-face!

FIRST CONVICT: I heard the warden's daughter married some guy from cell block D. The warden's really upset about it.
SECOND CONVICT: Why? Because she married a con?
FIRST CONVICT: No. Because they eloped!

221

How did they catch the crooks at the pig farm?

Someone squealed.

Why didn't the police arrest the runner?

She had a good track record.

Why did the police officers arrest the python after the accident?

It was a hiss and run.

...no hands on the steering wheel, not wearing a seatbelt, and half of you is riding in the back seat!

Why did the police investigate the seafood restaurant?

They knew something fishy was going on.

Why did the cops show up at the amusement park?

They heard somebody was being taken for a ride.

A cop stops a man who was speeding and asks, "Did you see the speed limit?"

The man replies, "Yes, I just didn't see you." ✩

The police were doing a suspect lineup and asked each man in the lineup to repeat the sentence "Give me all your money or I'll shoot."

The investigation ended a few seconds later when a man down the line screamed, "That's not what I said!" ✩

One night a police officer noticed a car that was traveling very slowly down the highway. When he pulled it over the driver asked, "What did I do wrong, officer?"

"You were going 26 miles per hour on a major highway. There is a law against that," the officer replied. "You have to go at least 50 miles per hour."

"But when I merged onto the highway, the sign said 26!" explained the driver.

The officer laughed and said, "That's because 26 is the name of the highway, not the speed limit!"

The driver leaned back in her seat, baffled, and the officer noticed another woman, extremely pale, sitting beside her. "What happened to her?" asked the officer.

"I'm not sure, but she's been like that ever since we got off of Highway 160." ✩

SPOTLIGHT

Diary of a Wimpy Kid

Jeff Kinney's bestselling *Diary of a Wimpy Kid* books originally began as a web comic in 2004. Though Kinney originally didn't intended to publish his story on the Internet, he realized that the opportunity to reach so many kids was too exciting a possibility to pass up. He posted new pieces of the story online in short installments every day, becoming more and more popular. Then in 2006 Kinney signed a multibook deal with a publisher, and in 2007 the *Diary of a Wimpy Kid* book series made its debut. It quickly became a *New York Times* bestseller, eventually reaching number 1.

There are seven books in the series so far, each following Greg Heffley and his struggles in middle school. Every book tackles new—and hilarious!—problems Greg must solve, including how to: use his best friend's popularity to his advantage; steer clear of the talent show and keep his nosy brother from revealing his biggest secret; convince his parents NOT to send him to a military academy; get out of "family togetherness" time; deal with boy-girl parties, increased responsibilities, and the awkwardness of growing up; and convince the grown-ups that he really isn't guilty of damaging school property (all while he's stuck in a cabin with his family).

In 2010, *Diary of a Wimpy Kid* was made into a movie. It was followed by a sequel, *Diary of a Wimpy Kid: Rodrick Rules* (2011), and the third installment, *Diary of a Wimpy Kid: Dog Days* (2012).

He might not know it, but with all this attention Greg Heffley might just be the most popular middle schooler around.

PRACTICAL JOKES

The Fruit Fake-Out: Convince your parents that their plants are growing fruit way out of season. Buy some beautiful, ripe pieces of fruit from the store and twist-tie them to the vines or branches.

The Face Trace: Mark the edge of a coin with soft pencil lead. Bet your friends that they can't roll the coin down their face and keep touching it at all times. They will be so eager to prove you wrong that they won't notice the line they have traced on their face.

The Spaghetti Sneeze: Help yourself to a small handful of plain cooked pasta. Hide it in your hand and pretend to sneeze just as you throw the gooey mass over your face or into someone's lap.

Cereal Sneakers: Leave dry cereal in the toes of your friend's shoes—add some crunch to someone's step!

Goofy Paint Trick: Go to the paint store and ask if you can buy striped paint.

The traffic cop pulls over a driver who has been speeding and asks him, "Didn't you see the speed limit signs posted on this road?"

"Why, officer," said the driver, "I was going much too fast to read those tiny little signs." ☆

How did the mutt defend his crime?

He blamed it on bad breeding.

Why couldn't the thunderclouds pull off the bank heist?

When the alarm went off, they all bolted.

Why was the comedian accused of assaulting her audience?

She gagged them and left them in stitches.

Why couldn't the cops catch the wallpaper thief?

There was a big cover-up.

How come the police didn't catch the woman who robbed the Laundromat?

She made a clean getaway.

A little old lady was speeding down the road while knitting. A cop caught up to her and, driving alongside her, shouted, "Pull over!"

"No," the little old lady replied. "They're mittens."

How did the runaway barber escape from the police?

He knew all the short cuts.

What do you call it when someone crashes into a police officer?

A run-in with the law!

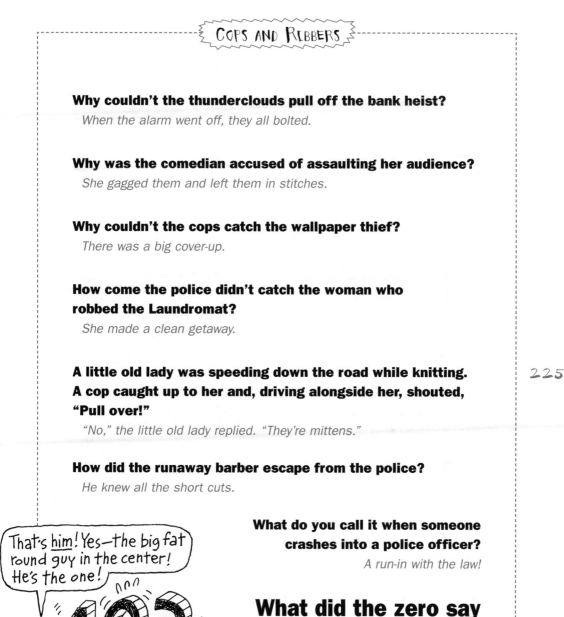

That's **him**! Yes—the big fat round guy in the center! He's the one!

What did the zero say when asked if he had committed the crime?

"I did nothing!"

BEHIND THE PUNCH LINE:
Hecklers

Stand-up comedy isn't always easy. Sometimes there are people in the audience called *hecklers* who don't think the comedian is funny or who don't think they're being entertained. A heckler will yell an insult at the comic, interrupting the monologue. A good comedian won't take the heckler seriously, and will yell something funny back, making everybody laugh. The best comedians will even get hecklers to laugh at themselves. The key is to stay cool—if you've rehearsed enough, then you won't be nervous—and play along. Improvisation techniques can be very helpful in dealing with hecklers. Take what they say and turn it into something funny. Your audience will think you're amazing!

How did the police know the blacksmith's signature was a fake?

It was forged.

Why didn't the police search for the missing rutabaga?

They knew it would turnip somewhere soon.

Why did the police raid the comic book store?

They were doing a strip search.

Why did the cops hang out at the coffee shop?

In case someone got mugged.

What do you get when you cross a SWAT team with an octopus?

A bomb squid.

What did the cops tell the mime when they arrested her?

"You still have the right to remain silent."

What did the police officer say when he caught the woman who had stolen the office equipment?

"Just give me the fax, ma'am."

Why were the charges against the football team dropped?

They had a strong defense.

> ## Thanksgiving Funnies:
>
> **Why were the Pilgrims' pants always falling down?**
> *They wore their belts around their hats.*

227

How did the police know the photographer was guilty?

They found his prints all over the scene of the crime.

Ooh, that smarts!

Did Sheriff Pat Garrett shoot Billy the Kid in the end?

No, he shot him right through the heart.

Why did the cops plant catnip at the scene of the crime?

To catch a cat burglar.

JUDGE: Order in the court!
DEFENDANT: I'll have a cheeseburger and fries, Your Honor.

JUDGE: I find you guilty and I'm giving you a choice: fifteen thousand dollars or six months in jail.
DEFENDANT: Your Honor, I'll take the money!

POLICE OFFICER (putting handcuffs on a crook): If I were you, I'd get myself a good lawyer.
CROOK: Officer, if I could afford a good lawyer, I wouldn't have tried to rob that bank.

A man walks into a convenience store with a gun and demands all the money in the cash register. After the cashier puts the money in a bag, the robber sees a bottle of whiskey that he wants on a shelf behind the counter. He tells the cashier to put it in the bag as well, but the cashier refuses saying, "You need to be over 21 to buy alcohol." The robber says he is, but the clerk still refuses to give the whiskey because he doesn't believe him.

After proving that he is over 21, the cashier puts the whiskey in the bag and the robber runs from the store.

A few minutes later, the cashier calls the police and gives them the robber's name and address. The officer who answered the phone asks, "How did you find out his name and address?"

"Simple," the cashier replies. "When I told him I didn't believe he was over 21, he gave me his ID to prove it." ☆

HOW MANY ELEPHANTS...

...Can You Fit in a Joke Book?

What happened to the elephant who had a nervous breakdown?

They had to give him trunquilizers.

Why do elephants have trunks?

Because they don't have glove compartments.

Why are elephants banned from public swimming pools?

They always drop their trunks.

Why are elephants so wrinkly?

They're too big to fit on the ironing board.

MAN: I'll bet you $100 that I can lift an elephant with one hand.
WOMAN: Ha! You're on!
MAN: Great! Go find me an elephant with one hand!

"Waiter!" yells a customer. "What's this elephant doing in my bowl of alphabet soup?"

The waiter comes over and says, "I suppose he's learning to read." ✩

What's gray, has wings, and gives money to baby elephants?

The tusk fairy.

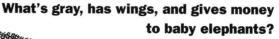

Hey—would you mind taking that hat off?

How do you know if there's an elephant in front of you at the movies?

You can't see the screen.

What do you get when you cross an elephant with an airplane?

A jumbo jet.

How do you capture an elephant?

Hide in the bushes and make peanut sounds.

What do you give an elephant with big feet?

Lots of room.

PRACTICAL JOKE

How to avoid going to bed:

• Wear plastic fangs and convince your parents that you're a vampire.

• Explain that the country has recently gone on Daylight Super-Saving Time, so it's actually only four o'clock in the afternoon. (Warning: This will work only in the summer!)

• Tell them that your science homework was to stay up and look for shooting stars, and that you'll flunk if you don't see at least one.

• Insist that you must stand guard all night in order to finally get that monster in your closet.

• Laugh and say, "I'm already in bed! You're just dreaming that I'm still awake!"

• Explain that you are practicing for New Year's Eve and have to stay up all night long.

231

A man was walking by a restaurant when he saw a sign in the window that read, "We will pay $100 to anyone who orders something we can't make." The man went inside and sat down, and when the waitress came over, he asked for an elephant sandwich. She dug in her apron, pulled out a roll of bills, and handed the man $100.

"What's the matter?" he asked. "No elephants today?"

"Oh, we have elephants, all right," she answered. "We're just all out of the big buns." ☆

Why did the elephant paint himself red and white?

So he could hide in a can of Coca-Cola.

What should you do for an elephant with an upset stomach?

Stay as far away from her as possible.

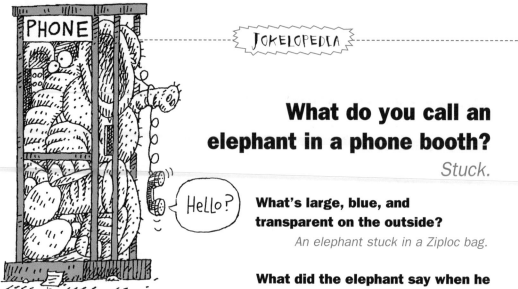

What do you call an elephant in a phone booth?

Stuck.

Hello?

What's large, blue, and transparent on the outside?

An elephant stuck in a Ziploc bag.

What did the elephant say when he walked into the post office?

"Ouch."

What time is it when an elephant sits on a fence?

Time to get a new fence.

232

What's large, gray, and wears a trench coat?

An undercover elephant.

What's the difference between an elephant and a cookie?

Have you ever tried dunking an elephant in milk?

Why was the vacationing elephant so glum?

The airline lost his trunk.

Why do elephants have big trunks?

So they have somewhere to put the groceries when they go shopping.

What do you call an elephant on the run?

An earthquake.

Jason Segel

Jason Segel got his start on TV in the short-lived comedy-drama series *Freaks and Geeks* (1999–2000). Though the show lasted only one season, it was enough to get him noticed. After starring in another short-lived TV series, *Undeclared* (2001–2002), he finally found a long-term home in 2005 on the hit TV comedy series *How I Met Your Mother*. He plays Marshall Eriksen, an optimistic, environmentally conscious lawyer. The series is critically acclaimed, having won six Emmy Awards and the 2012 People's Choice Award for Best TV Network Comedy.

Segel has also starred in numerous comedy films. His first appearance was in the 2007 blockbuster hit *Knocked Up*. He later went on to write and star in the hilarious hit *Forgetting Sarah Marshall* (2008), in which Segel's character, Peter, goes to Hawaii in order to get over his recent breakup with his famous girlfriend, Sarah Marshall. Unbeknownst to him, she is at the same resort with her new boyfriend. The movie proved him to be not only a great actor but also a talented writer.

After the success of *Forgetting Sarah Marshall*, Segel went on to star in another smash hit, *I Love You, Man* (2009), alongside Paul Rudd. The movie follows Peter (Rudd) in his attempt to find a male friend. He eventually meets Sydney (Segel), and the two form a very tight and hilarious "bromance."

Segel went on to star in and write *The Muppets* (2011), the first Muppets movie in twelve years, and a huge box-office hit. Though he started his career out as a "freak," he developed into a very talented actor and writer.

What is big and gray and protects you from the rain?

An umbrellephant.

What goes up slowly and down quickly?

An elephant in an elevator.

What do you call an elephant wearing ear muffs?

Anything you want—he can't hear you!

What do you get when you cross a parrot with an elephant?

An animal that repeats everything it remembers.

What's the difference between a *Tyrannosaurus rex* and an elephant?

One dismembers; the other remembers.

234

What's the difference between a skateboard and an elephant?

One has four wheels; the other doesn't.

Where do you find an elephant?

Wherever you left her.

Why did the elephant leave the circus?

He was tired of working for peanuts.

Why don't elephants like elephant jokes?

They think they're Dumbo.

Where do elephants go to see art?

The peanut gallery.

What's the difference between an elephant and a loaf of bread?

If you don't know, then let's hope no one ever sends you to the corner store to buy a loaf of bread!

Why did the elephant forget?

She didn't renew her remembership.

What's the world's largest ant?

An eleph-ant.

What is big and gray and lost its glass slipper?

Cinderelephant.

What's small and pink?

An elephant's tutu.

What's old, gray, and wrinkled?

A stale raisin pretending to be an elephant.

What do you get when you cross an elephant with a ghost?

Wrinkled sheets.

How do you make an elephant laugh?

Tickle him.

235

THE MAKING OF A COMEDIAN

Step 7: Don't Give It All Away!

Shhhh! We didn't just give these jokes away, did we? Well, neither should you. Never, ever blurt out a punch line before its time. You shouldn't ask people if they've heard the joke before, because you might give yourself away in the process. A funny joke is like a well-planned surprise party—the bigger the surprise, the happier the party.

236

Why did the elephant fall out of the tree?

Because it lost its balance.

So why did the second elephant fall out of the tree?

It was stuck to the first one.

Then why did the third elephant fall out of the tree?

It thought the other two were playing a game.

And why did the tree fall down?

It wanted to be an elephant. ☆

What steps would you take if you were being chased by an elephant?

Very big, quick ones.

What should you do with an elephant in a cast?

Make sure she knows her lines.

What's an elephant's favorite card game?

Memory.

DAUGHTER: Why is a snail stronger than an elephant?
MOTHER: I don't know. Why?
DAUGHTER: Because a snail can carry its own home, while an elephant can only carry its own trunk.

What's large, gray, and goes up and down?

An elephant in an exercise class.

What's large, gray, and hard to spot?

A stain-resistant elephant.

Why do elephants drive Volkswagens?

There's room for four and the rest is trunk space.

How can you tell if there's an elephant in your bag of Oreos?

Read the list of ingredients.

How do you know there's an elephant in the bottom of your bunk bed?

Your nose touches the ceiling.

How do you stop an elephant from charging?

Take away his credit card!

Why are elephants known to hold grudges?

They can forgive, but they can't forget.

So, YOU'RE the doctor who slapped me when I was born!

How do you tell if there's an elephant in your refrigerator?

There are footprints in the butter.

How can you tell when there are two elephants in your refrigerator?

You can hear them giggling.

238

How can you tell when there are three elephants in your refrigerator?

The door won't close.

How can you tell when there are four elephants in your refrigerator?

The light is on and there's a Volkswagen parked outside.

Why don't elephants like computers?

They're afraid of the mouse.

What do you call an elephant on a bike?

Wheelie dangerous.

Why did the elephant go running?

It wanted to jog its memory.

Knock, knock.
Who's there?
Gladys.
Gladys who?
Gladys you and not another elephant joke!

MONSTER-OSITIES

Ghouls, Goblins, and the Like

What do celebrity vampires receive?

Fang mail.

What do you get when alien teenagers invade shopping malls on Earth?

Clothes encounters of the third kind.

What should you do to keep a corpse from smelling?

Nothing, silly. Dead people can't smell!

Where did the vampire open his savings account?

At the blood bank.

I'm savink zis for a sunny day...

FIRST BOY: Why do you keep throwing garlic cloves out of your window?
SECOND BOY: To keep away the vampires.
FIRST BOY: But there are no vampires.
SECOND BOY: Then it must be working!

A young boy goes in for an operation to remove a monster he accidentally swallowed. The doctor puts him to sleep and goes to operate. When the boy wakes up, the doctor is holding a giant green monster. "Nothing to worry about," the doctor says. "The operation was a success. We got the monster out."

"No, you didn't," the boy replies. "The one I swallowed was blue!" ☆

240

What's a werewolf's favorite day of the week?

Moonday.

Two dragons are chasing a knight in armor. Just as they are about to catch him, the first dragon says, "You remembered to bring the barbecue sauce this time, right?"

The second dragon answers, "Yes. And I hope you remembered the can opener." ☆

Okay, stay right there while I get the salad...

Why don't vampires kiss people?

They've got bat breath.

What do you get when you cross a witch with ice?

A cold spell.

Did you hear about the two mind readers who met on the street?

The first one said, "Well, you're fine. How am I?"

What kind of TV do you find in a haunted house?

A big-scream TV.

At what time did Dracula go to the dentist?

Tooth hurty.

BAD JOKE BREAK

Exasperate a friend! You say the lines in bold; the lines after the bold lines are answers your friend will most likely give. The most important thing about this trick is to go on long enough so that your friend is confident with her answers. Then you make her groan when you get to the trick at the end!

What's red and goes "ding dong"?
I don't know—what?

A red ding dong. What's blue and goes "ding dong"?
A blue ding dong?

Right! What's green and goes "ding dong"?
A green ding dong?

Right again. Now, what's purple and goes "ding dong"?
Why, that must be a purple ding dong.

Correct. And what's pink and goes "ding dong"?
A pink ding dong?

Nope. They don't come in pink.

241

Why are graveyards so popular?

Because everyone's dying to get in.

Why was there no food left after the Halloween party?

Because everyone was goblin.

Why did the cannibal get suspended from school?

He was caught buttering up his teacher.

What did the zombie's friend say when he introduced him to his girlfriend?

"Good grief! Where did you dig her up from?"

What do you say to an angry monster?

"Gosh, no need to bite my head off."

242

A woman walked into a bar with a big, vicious-looking monster on a leash.

"Sorry, madam," said the bartender, "but that creature looks dangerous. You'll have to tie him up outside."

The woman took the monster outside, then came back and ordered a drink. She was just finishing it when a man came into the bar and said, "Whose monster is that outside?"

"Mine," said the woman proudly.

"Well, I'm sorry," the man said, "but my dog just killed your monster."

"Killed him! What kind of dog do you have?"

"A miniature poodle," said the man.

"But how could a miniature poodle kill my great big monster?"

"She got stuck in his throat and choked him!" ☆

A girl was walking in the dark one night when she heard a bump bump bump bump behind her. She started moving faster, but the bump bump bump bump continued. When she turned around, she was startled to notice a giant coffin bouncing over in her direction. Frightened, the girl began to run with all her might. To her horror, the coffin just went *bump bump bump bump* faster and faster. She ran and ran all the way to her home, through the front gate, up the path, and up the steps to her door where, after a great deal of struggling with the keys, she finally managed to unlock the door, get inside, and lock the door behind her. But just as she got inside, the coffin came crashing through her front door and chased her up the staircase! She ran and locked herself into the bathroom. The girl was totally exhausted by now, almost crying, when the coffin smashed through her bathroom door. Determined to survive, she groped around the room for anything she could find to save herself, but all she found was a bottle of cough syrup in the medicine cabinet. Desperate, she threw the cough syrup at the coffin.

And the coffin stopped. ☆

What do you call a person who puts poison in someone's corn flakes?

A cereal killer.

What can you find between Godzilla's toes?

Slow runners.

What kind of monster loves to dance?

The boogieman.

What is the largest building in Transylvania?

The Vampire State Building.

243

What do you say if the Abominable Snowman is about to chomp your head off?

"Chill, dude."

Chill, Dude!

Why is it good to tell ghost stories in hot weather?

Because they are so chilling.

What do squirrels say on Halloween?

"Trick or tree."

What does Tweety Bird say on Halloween?

"Twick or tweet."

What do diplomats say on Halloween?

"Trick or treaty."

Where do you go when a ghost is chasing you?

The living room.

How do you make a witch itch?

Take away her W.

BOY: I'll stop being frightened if you'll stop being scared.
GIRL: That sounds like a fear trade to me.

R. L. Stine and Goosebumps

Robert Lawrence (R. L. to his fans) Stine, the author of the wildly popular series *Goosebumps*, began writing stories when he was nine years old. An avid comic book reader as a kid, he especially enjoyed the scary ones like *Tales from the Crypt* and *Vault of Horror*. Stine says those comic books strongly influenced the writing in his own scary stories. "When I write, I try to think back to what I was afraid of or what was scary to me, and try to put those feelings into

books," he says. *Goosebumps* was also a popular TV show in the late '90s. And in 2012, Stine began publishing short horror stories on Twitter, 140 characters at a time. The *Goosebumps* film series launched in 2015.

Stine once edited a joke magazine called *Bananas* under the name Jovial Bob. As Jovial Bob, he also wrote several joke books, including *101 Silly Monster Jokes* and *Bozos on Patrol*. He says his background as a funnyman helps him because he knows what will make kids laugh, as well as what will scare them. This sixth sense for kids' book tastes has earned him the nickname "the children's Stephen King." Combining giggles with ghouls makes *Goosebumps* stories that much more enjoyable! In fact, Stine says the best way to be a writer of any kind is to have a broad reading background. After all, the more you read, the more things you'll know about that you can write about!

Tarzan was swinging along his vines when he suddenly found himself surrounded by terrible monsters. Vampires, werewolves, abominable snowmen, goblins, witches, and more. Do you know what he said?

"Boy, am I ever in the wrong joke." ☆

A very pompous man was walking around an art exhibit, critiquing every piece he came across. After a while, he came to stop at a particular exhibit and asked the owner, "Is this picture of a hideous monster what you call modern art these days?"

"No, sir," the owner said. "It's what we call a mirror." ☆

What's a monster's favorite snack?
Ghoul scout cookies.

What monster has the best hearing?
The eeriest.

Did you hear the one about the vampire?
It was a vein attempt at humor.

Did you hear about the poor vampire slayer?
He tried to kill a vampire by driving a pork chop through its heart because a steak was too expensive.

Why didn't the skeleton cross the road?
Because he didn't have the guts.

Why don't witches ride on their brooms when they're angry?

How do vampires get around on Halloween night?

By blood vessels.

Did you hear about the monster with eight arms?

He said they came in handy.

Who wins at zombie baseball games?

Nobody. It's always dead even.

What happened to the guy who couldn't keep up on the payments to his exorcist?

He was re-possessed.

What is Transylvania?

Dracula's terror-tory.

Why should a skeleton drink lots of milk?

It's good for the bones.

Where do zombies go for a swim?

The Dead Sea.

Why can you tell mummies secrets?

They're good at keeping things under wraps.

How do you get to a monster's house?

Take a fright at the dead end.

They're afraid of flying off the handle.

Where does Dracula water ski?

On Lake Eerie.

Who won the skeleton beauty contest?

No body.

What do skeletons say before they start to eat?

"Bone appétit!"

Where do baby ghosts go during the day?

To a day-scare center.

Why are most monsters covered in wrinkles?

Have you ever tried to iron a monster?

248

AAHH...

Who did Frankenstein take to the prom?

His ghoul-friend.

What do ghosts serve for dessert?

Ice scream.

Seinfeld

A show about nothing? That's exactly what *Seinfeld* is. It follows the life of comedian Jerry Seinfeld and his neurotic and crazy friends: Kramer, George, and Elaine. Episodes from the early seasons were inspired by everyday events from the life of cocreator Larry David. A typical episode sees each character through a series of absurd but somehow believable events and wraps with each of the storylines coming together in the end. The show was on the air for nine hilarious seasons, and is one of the most popular syndicated shows of all time. Ever hear anyone say "yadda, yadda, yadda" or call someone "man hands," a "close talker," or a "mimbo"? *Seinfeld* introduced the world to all of these phrases. For a show about nothing, it certainly provides many laughs!

What do witches put in their hair?

Scare spray.

What do you call a haunted chicken?

A poultry-geist.

What kind of mistakes do ghosts make?

Boo boos.

What's a monster's favorite play?

Romeo and Ghouliet.

What do you get when you cross Bambi with a ghost?

Bamboo.

Eye of Newt makes great sunscreen!

What would you find on a haunted beach?

A sand witch.

What do goblins and ghosts drink when they're hot and thirsty?

Ghoul-Aid.

What is a vampire's favorite holiday?

Fangsgiving.

What's it like to be kissed by a vampire?

It's a pain in the neck.

256

A monster is devouring an entire football team. Another monster comes along and argues that he's eating more than his share. "Okay," the first monster says. "I'll give you halfback." ☆

Why don't mummies take vacations?

They're afraid they'll relax and unwind.

What would you get if you crossed a Spaniel, a French poodle, a ghost, and a rooster?

A cocker-poodle-boo!

When do ghosts usually appear?

Just before someone screams.

The Addams Family

The "mysterious and spooky, altogether ooky" Addams family began as a series of cartoons drawn by Charles Addams for *The New Yorker* magazine from 1932 until his death in 1988. In the early 1960s, a TV producer created a show based on Addams's drawings. The main characters were Gomez and Morticia Addams; their children, Pugsley and Wednesday; Uncle Fester; Lurch, the butler; and lovable Cousin Itt.

In 1991, a movie called *The Addams Family* came out, followed by a sequel, *Addams Family Values*, in 1993. The movies introduced Addams's characters to a whole new generation, along with the familiar theme song (snap, snap). The appeal of the Addams family was that they didn't seem to realize their own freakiness—making their encounters with the world outside their creepy mansion (with its own graveyard) all the funnier. Remember little Wednesday in the first film, asking whether the Girl Scout cookies contained real Girl Scouts?

What do you call the ghost of a door-to-door salesperson?

A dead ringer.

Why do dragons sleep during the day?

So they can fight knights.

Why do witches think they're funny?

Every time they look in the mirror, it cracks up.

How do you make a strawberry shake?

Sneak up behind it and yell "BOO!"

252

What happens when a flying witch breaks the sound barrier?

You hear the broom boom.

Hey—what happened to the catbox and the Kitty Litter?

I ate them...

Why did the other kids have to let the vampire play baseball?

It was his bat.

What do you call an overweight pumpkin?

A plumpkin.

What do you get when you cross a monster with a cat?

A mew-tation.

How do mummies hide?

They wear masking tape.

What kind of dog does Dracula have?

A bloodhound.

Where does Count Dracula wash his hair?

In the bat tub.

Knock, knock.
Who's there?
Ivanna.
Ivanna who?
Ivanna suck your blood.

253

Why did the vampire's girlfriend dump him?

The relationship was too draining.

Why did Count Dracula see his doctor?

He was always coffin.

Why did the vampire run screaming out of the restaurant?

He found out it was a stake house.

What do you call a bloodthirsty Philadelphian?

A Pennsylvanian Transylvanian.

Where do you store a werewolf?

In a were-house.

What does a ghost eat for lunch?

A boo-logna sandwich.

What kind of fur do you get from a werewolf?

As fur away as possible.

What should you do when you find a ghost in your living room?

Offer him a sheet.

What should you do with overweight ghosts?

Exorcize them.

Knock, knock.
Who's there?
Voodoo.
Voodoo who?
Voodoo you think you are?

How do ghosts get to school in the morning?

They take a ghoul bus.

254

PATIENT: Doctor, you have to help me!
DOCTOR: What's wrong?
PATIENT: Every night I dream about terrible monsters under my bed. What should I do?
DOCTOR: Saw the legs off your bed.

SALLY: A monster bit my arm!
JAKE: Which one?
SALLY: I'm not sure. All those monsters look the same to me!

How does a monster count to 142?

On its fingers.

What do you call a witch who loves the beach but won't go in the water?

A chicken sand-witch.

What do you do with a green monster?

Wait until he ripens.

What do you do with a blue monster?

Try to cheer him up.

Why don't monsters eat clowns?

They taste funny.

What do ghost babies wear on their feet?

Boo-tees!

What has a broom and flies?

A jelly-covered janitor.

Why do ghouls and demons hang out together?

Because demons are a ghoul's best friend.

255

What do you call a nervous witch?

A twitch.

What do you get when you cross a snowman with a vampire?

Frostbite.

Why wasn't the girl afraid of the monster?

It was a man-eating monster.

What do you call a giant monster who lives in the ocean and makes loud noises when he drinks?

A sea slurpant.

What giant monster lives in the mountains and hems men's suits?

The abominable sew-man.

Why don't abominable snowmen ever marry?

They always get cold feet.

256

What do you call a large gorilla who likes to dance?

King Conga.

We dare you to try this spooky, slippery tongue twister three times fast: Which witch watched which witch's watch walk?

Why did the ghoul cry when her pet zombie ran away?

Because he ran off with her mummy.

Why couldn't the young witch find a job?

She didn't have enough hex-perience.

How can you tell when two monsters are getting along?

Why did the wizard drop out of school?

He couldn't spell.

Why didn't the two four-eyed monsters marry?

Because they could never see eye to eye to eye to eye.

Why did the little skeleton feel left out?

He had no body to play with.

257

Why don't skeletons go bungee jumping?

Because they don't have any guts.

How did Frankenstein know he was in love?

He felt that certain spark.

Why did the Blob stay home on Saturday night?

He was all dressed up with nowhere to goo.

They see eye to eye to eye to eye to eye to eye to eye to eye.

A vampire bat came flapping in from the night covered in fresh blood, and parked himself on the roof of the cave to get some sleep. Pretty soon all the other bats smelled the blood and began asking him where he got it. He told them to knock it off and let him get some sleep, but they persisted until finally he gave in. "OK, follow me," he said, and flew out of the cave with hundreds of bats behind him. Down through a valley they went, across a river, and into a forest full of trees. Finally he slowed down and all the other bats excitedly milled around him. "Now, do you see that tree over there?" he asked. "Yes, yes, yes!" the bats all screamed in a frenzy. "Good," said the first bat. "Because I *didn't!*" ✩

Why did Godzilla visit New York on Saturday evening?

He wanted a night out on the town.

Say-these taste great! Crunchy with a creamy filling!

REALLY OLD JOKES

Extinct Animals and Funny Fossils

Where did *Tyrannosaurus rex* live?
Anywhere it wanted to.

Why aren't there any dinosaurs in animal crackers?
Because they're extinct, silly! And anyway, they wouldn't fit in the box.

What would you get if you crossed a dinosaur with a pig?
Jurassic Pork.

What is a *T. rex*'s favorite number?
8.

What do you get when you cross a *T. rex* with some fireworks?
Dino-mite.

What do you call a fossil that never works?
Lazy bones.

What do you call a *T. rex* that has nothing interesting to say?

A dino-bore.

What do you call a *T. rex* that gets the winning goal?

A dino-score.

Did you hear the rumor about the dinosaur that terrorized Florida?

It was a croc.

How do you know when a dinosaur has gone bad?

Check her expiration date.

What do you get when you cross a prehistoric animal with a cat?

A 'saur-puss.

260

What music do hip dinosaurs listen to?

Raptor music.

THUN-KA
THUN-KA
THUN-KA
THUN-KA

What's the difference between a pterodactyl and a chicken?

When you come down with a cold, nobody ever offers you a bowl of hot pterodactyl soup.

What's the difference between a pterodactyl and a parrot?

You'd know the answer if you ever let a pterodactyl sit on your shoulder.

What's the difference between a pterodactyl and a turkey?

The drumsticks are bigger on a pterodactyl.

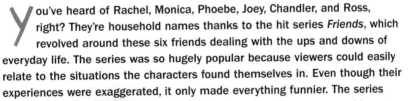

Uh, 'scuse me... could I get a bigger fork?

Where do pterodactyls park their cars?

In Jurassic parking lots.

What do dinosaurs have that no other animal has?

Baby dinosaurs.

Which dinosaur sleeps all day?

The dino-snore.

261

Friends

You've heard of Rachel, Monica, Phoebe, Joey, Chandler, and Ross, right? They're household names thanks to the hit series *Friends*, which revolved around these six friends dealing with the ups and downs of everyday life. The series was so hugely popular because viewers could easily relate to the situations the characters found themselves in. Even though their experiences were exaggerated, it only made everything funnier. The series debuted in 1994, ran for 10 seasons, and is one of the most highly syndicated shows on television today. At the time it was on the air, the show was a huge pop-culture hit as well, introducing "the Rachel" hairdo and catchphrases "How you doin'?" and "on a break."

How do you know there's a brontosaurus in the house?

The cheese is missing from the mousetraps.

How do you know there's a tyrannosaurus in the house?

The brontosaurus is missing.

What do you call it when a tyrannosaurus throws a brontosaurus at another tyrannosaurus?

Food fight!

Where did the dodo bird like to fly for his winter vacation?

Nowhere—dodoes couldn't fly.

Why did the first fish grow legs and walk out of the ocean?

He had to go to the bathroom.

When do dinosaurs put on bandages?

When they get dino-sores.

Who puts braces on woolly mammoths?

The mastodontist.

Why did the brontosaurus climb into the active volcano?

He wasn't very smart.

What did the stegosaurus say to the cute brontosaurus at the tar pit?

"Hey, I'm glad you decided to stick around."

BEHIND THE PUNCH LINE:
Classic Comedy

Good comedy is all about pleasing the audience. Take William Shakespeare, for example. Usually, we think of Shakespeare's plays as difficult academic works. But Shakespeare's comedic plays, such as *The Taming of the Shrew, As You Like It,* and *Twelfth Night,* are uproariously funny and loaded with plays on words, silly characters, and loads of comic situations. The playwright's tragedies are masterpieces of the English language, too. Many of our sayings come directly from Shakespeare, in fact. Shakespeare wrote for the people— he consciously avoided the stiff, snobby style of other writers in order to please the people in the theater.

263

When did cave people invest hockey?

During the ice age.

If a triceratops and a pebble are standing on the edge of a cliff, which one jumps first?

The pebble—it's a little boulder.

What kind of shoes do dinosaurs wear?

Triceratops.

What does a triceratops sit on?

Its tricera-bottom.

Which dinosaur roamed the wild, wild west?

Tyrannosaurus Tex.

And what did he ride?

A bronco-saurus.

Where does a *T. rex* buy clothes?

A dino-store.

How do you brush a saber-toothed tiger's teeth?

Very carefully.

Why did the dinosaurs become extinct?

Because they wouldn't take a bath.

What's louder than a dinosaur?

A whole bunch of dinosaurs.

What do you get when you turn a dinosaur upside down?

A triceratops-y turvy.

What kind of material do dinosaurs use for the floors of their homes?

Rep-tiles.

Where does the *T. rex* go for vacation?
The dino-shore.

Why do museums only have old bones?
Because they can't afford new ones!

What is the scariest dinosaur?
Terror-dactyl.

ha-ha!

What kind of accidents do dinosaurs get into?
Tyrannosaurus wrecks.

What do you call a reptile who hangs out in bars?
A lounge lizard.

265

What's round, covered with chocolate, and tastes like a wooly mammoth?
A masto-donut.

Why did the Apatosaurus have the factory for dinner?
Because she was a plant eater!

KNOCK-KNOCKS

Knock, knock.
Who's there?
Banana.
Banana who?
Knock, knock.
Who's there?
Banana.
Banana who?
Knock, knock.
Who's there?
———

Banana.
Banana who?
Knock, knock.
Who's there?
Orange.
Orange who?
Orange you glad I didn't
    say "banana"?

Knock, knock.
Who's there?
Police.
Police who?
Po-lice open the door!
———

Knock, knock.
Who's there?
Deluxe.
Deluxe who?
Deluxe-smith. I'm here to fix de lock.
———

Knock, knock.
Who's there?
Honey bee.
Honey bee who?
Honey bee a dear and get me some tea.
———

Knock, knock.
Who's there?
Hatch.
Hatch who?
Bless you!

Knock, knock.
Who's there?
Kanga.
Kanga who?
No, kangaroo!
———

Knock, knock.
Who's there?
Doris.
Doris who?
Doris locked. That's why I knocked!
———

Knock, knock.
Who's there?
Polo.
Polo who?
Polo-ver, you're under arrest.

Knock, knock.
Who's there?
Xena.
Xena who?
Xena good movie lately?
———

Knock, knock.
Who's there?
IBM.
IBM who?
IBM. Who be you?

Knock, knock.

Who's there?

Anita.

Anita who?

Anita nother minute to think it over.

——

Knock, knock.

Who's there?

Electra.

Electra who?

Electricity. Isn't that shocking?

——————

Knock, knock.

Who's there?

Omelet.

Omelet who?

Omelet smarter than I sound.

——

Knock, knock.

Who's there?

Thor.

Thor who?

Thorry, wrong door.

——

Knock, knock.

Who's there?

Justin.

Justin who?

Justin time for dinner!

——

Knock, knock.

Who's there?

Usher.

Usher who?

Usher wish you'd let me in!

Knock, knock.

Who's there?

Raven.

Raven who?

Raven lunatic who wants to knock down your door!

——

Knock, knock.

Who's there?

Little old lady.

Little old lady who?

Wow, I didn't know you could yodel!

——

Knock, knock.

Who's there?

Byte.

Byte who?

Byte you're happy to see me again.

——

Knock, knock.

Who's there?

DOS.

DOS who?

DOS your computer have an operating system?

267

Knock, knock.

Who's there?

Cow go.

Cow go who?

No, cow go moo.

Knock, knock.

Who's there?

Huron.

Huron who?

Huron my toe, could you please step off it?

Knock, knock.

Who's there?

Lotus.

Lotus who?

Lotus in and we'll tell you.

Knock, knock.

Who's there?

Comma.

Comma who?

Comma little closer and I'll kiss you.

Knock, knock.

Who's there?

Alaska.

Alaska who?

Alaska 'nother person if you don't know the answer.

Knock, knock.

Who's there?

Sparrow.

Sparrow who?

Sparrow me the details and let me in.

Knock, knock.

Who's there?

Wire.

Wire who?

Wire you asking me that again. I just told you!

Will you remember me in an hour?

Yes.

Will you remember me in a day?

Yes.

Will you remember me in a week?

Yes.

Will you remember me in a month?

Yes.

Will you remember me in a year?

Yes.

I think you won't.

Yes, I will.

Knock, knock.

Who's there?

See? You've forgotten me already!

268

ha-ha!

TONGUE TWISTERS

Try these totally tasteless tongue twisters:

Sick Suzy sucks slimy snot.

Can canned clams can clams?

The fifth fink sinks faster than the first four finks think.

Such a silly tongue twister mustn't be mumbled.

Feeble felines fear fur.

Sneaking in my creaky squeaky reeking sneakers.

Betty better butter Buddy's bread.

A cheeky chipmunk chucked cheap chocolate chips in the cheap chocolate-chip store.

I'm hooked on the book Brooke brought back from the Brookside bookstore.

Kent sent Trent the rent to rent Trent's tent.

Sally saw Shelley singing swinging summer swimming songs.

The corn on the cob made Bob the Slob's sobbing stop.

The ocean sure soaked Sherman.

Can you say these three times fast?

She freed six sick sheep.

She freed three shy sheep.

269

RECORD YOUR OWN JOKES

RECORD YOUR OWN JOKES

RECORD YOUR OWN JOKES

RECORD YOUR OWN JOKES

RECORD YOUR OWN JOKES

RECORD YOUR OWN JOKES

PHOTO CREDITS

Page 9: Mary Ellen Matthews/NBC/NBCU Photo Bank/Getty Images

Page 45: Jason LaVeris/Getty Images

Page 52: Photo by Taylor Hill/WireImage/Getty Images

Page 57: Universal Studios/Photofest

Page 67: NBC/Photofest

Page 79: Donna Ward/Getty Images

Page 93: Barry King/Getty Images

Page 103: Toni Passig/Getty Images

Page 117: bottom, Ray Jones/Getty Images; top, RKO Radio Pictures/Photofest

Page 129: Jason Merritt/Getty Images

Page 145: Columbia Pictures/Photofest

Page 149: Alo Ceballos/Getty Images

Page 162: Columbia Pictures/Photofest

Page 166: Photofest

Page 171: Fox/Photofest

Page 181: Nickelodeon/Photofest

Page 191: Universal Studios/Photofest

Page 211: CBS/Photofest

Page 213: Nickelodeon/Photofest

Page 223: Photofest/Twentieth Century-Fox Film Corporation

Page 233: Ray Tamarra/Getty Images

Page 245: Ben Gabbe/Getty Images

Page 249: NBC/Photofest

Page 261: Warner Bros./Photofest